Grand Diplôme® Cooking Course

Volume15

Grand Diplôme® Cooking Course

A Danbury Press Book

The Danbury Press

a division of Grolier Enterprises, Inc.

Robert B. Clarke   Publisher

This book has been adapted from the Grand Diplôme Cooking Course, originally published by Purnell Cookery, U.S.A.

Purnell Grand Diplôme Editorial Board

Rosemary Hume and Muriel Downes
Principals, London Cordon Bleu Cookery
School, England

Anne Willan	Editor
Eleanor Noderer	Associate Editor
Sheryl Julian	Assistant Editor
John Paton	Managing Editor
José Northey	Co-ordinating Editor
Peter Leather	Art Editor
Charles F. Turgeon	Wine Consultant
Joy Langridge	Consultant Editor

Library of Congress Catalog Card Number: 72-13896
© Phoebus Publishing Company/BPC Publishing
Limited, 1971/1972/1979
Filmsetting by Petty and Sons Ltd., Leeds, England.
Printed in the United States of America

4567899

All recipes have been tested either at the Cordon Bleu Cookery School in London or in our U.S. test kitchens.

Note: all recipe quantities in this book serve 4 people unless otherwise stated.

Contents

From the Editor

Braised veal Orloff, named for a Russian aristocrat, and tiny squabs bonne femme, simmered with bacon and baby onions are among the cooking classics you will meet in the **Menus** of Volume 15 of your Grand Diplôme Cooking Course. For a special celebration, the Cordon Bleu Cookery School of London has designed **Wedding Menus** for gatherings large and small. Equally elegant are the **Cakes for Special Occasions** that range from a snowy tub of ladyfingers filled with little meringue mushrooms to a rococo basket of flowers, overflowing with crimson marzipan roses. Less intricate but just as luxurious are **Sophisticated Quick Dishes** like lobster omelet Barante and truffle-topped tournedos Rossini.

A delicious ramekin of crab topped with aspic, and a pâté of potted shrimp are just part of the immense collection of **Cold Hors d'Oeuvre and Appetizers.** You'll be equally inspired by the unusual **Salads for Light Lunches**, where mushrooms are combined with cheese, pineapple with tarragon and veal with green pepper. Century-old recipes make up the second feature on **Classic Entrées** that are perfect for today's entertaining. And for original cooking ideas, explore such delights as a Roquefort mousse or a Swiss cheese fondue as you acquire the know-how of **Cooking with Cheese.** You'll also find suggestions for **Garnishes**, and decorating **Easter Eggs.**

A whole new world awaits you in the **Cooking of Mexico** — hot, pungent chilies in fiery reds and glorious greens, the basic bean in a collage of colors from gold and pink to black, the robust texture of finely-ground nuts combines with zesty herbs and spices in dishes guaranteed to add life to any meal. You'll learn the t's and q's of Mexican cooking from tortillas, tostadas, tacos and tamales to quesadillas and, in the process, you'll find that preparation is twice as easy as pronunciation.

Buen Apetito!

Anne Willan.

Here is a menu for a luxury wedding lunch. Quantities are enough for 12 people, and the timetable gives detailed instructions on how to prepare in advance for the great day.

The idea that Champagne is suitable for every dish on any occasion is not strictly correct. But there are occasions — none more appropriate than a wedding — when all dishes seem ideally complemented by this festive, effervescent wine. The only real Champagne comes from the district of the same name in northeastern France and can, therefore, be expensive. Less costly but equally pleasant sparkling wines are available from the Touraine region of France as well as from California and New York. As your choice of wine must run the course from aspic to chocolate, it is probably best to select an extra dry Champagne or other sparkling wine.

STUFF TURKEY WITH TRUFFLES FOR A LUXURY WEDDING LUNCH

Turkey en Gelée

Celery & Green Pepper Chartreuse

Green Salad

Peach and Hazelnut Galette

∽∾

Champagne or other Sparkling Wine

◀*Turkey en gelée has tartlets filled with cranberry sauce arranged around it; serve celery and green pepper chartreuse separately (recipes are on pages 10–11)*

TIMETABLE

Day before
Roast turkey and keep covered in refrigerator. Prepare aspic for bird and cover.
Make the celery and green pepper chartreuses, cover with plastic wrap and refrigerate.
Make and bake galette rounds; store, layered, in wax paper in a plastic bag; make chocolate rounds for galettes and store in cool place.
Prepare mousse for turkey; complete turkey en gelée but do not set on platter; store, covered, including chopped aspic for platter, in refrigerator.
Wash watercress and salad greens and store in plastic bag in refrigerator. Make vinaigrette dressing for green salad and store in screwtop jar.
Make and bake tartlet shells and store in airtight container.

Morning
Chill cranberry sauce.
Arrange assorted breads, rolls and crackers and cover tightly with plastic wrap.
Combine greens in salad bowl, cover and refrigerate.
Make Chantilly cream for galettes.
Peel, pit and slice fresh peaches or drain canned peaches and add to Chantilly cream. Complete galettes and chill.
Chill wine in refrigerator about 1 hour before serving.

Just before serving
Set turkey on bed of chopped aspic, fill tartlet shells with cranberry sauce and arrange around bird, cover and keep in refrigerator.
Unmold celery and green pepper chartreuses and garnish centers with watercress.
Toss salad with dressing.

> You will find that **cooking times** given in the individual recipes for these dishes have sometimes been adapted in the timetable to help you when cooking and serving this menu as a buffet.

Entrée

Turkey en Gelée

10–12 lb turkey
1 medium onion, stuck with 1 clove
6 tablespoons butter
$\frac{3}{4}$–1 cup stock
$\frac{1}{4}$ cup sherry

For mousse
1$\frac{1}{2}$ lb cooked ham
1 cup butter, softened
thick béchamel sauce, made with 3 tablespoons butter, 3 tablespoons flour and 1$\frac{1}{2}$ cups milk (infused with slice of onion, 6 peppercorns, blade of mace and bay leaf)
$\frac{3}{4}$ cup heavy cream, whipped until it holds a soft shape
$\frac{1}{2}$ lb cooked tongue, shredded
liquid from truffle (see garnish)
salt and pepper

For garnish
4 cups cool but still liquid chicken aspic
1 canned truffle, sliced (reserve the liquid for mousse)
10–12 baked tartlet shells, made with 1 cup quantity rich pie pastry
1 can (8 oz) strained or whole cranberry sauce

Trussing needle and string

Method
Set oven at moderately hot (375°F).
Put the onion stuck with the clove and 2 tablespoons butter in the cavity of the bird and truss it. Place bird in a roasting pan and pour around $\frac{3}{4}$ cup stock and the sherry; melt remaining butter and pour over the bird. Cover it loosely with foil and roast in the heated oven for $2\frac{3}{4}$–$3\frac{1}{4}$ hours or until a meat thermo-meter inserted in the thickest part of the thigh registers 185°F.

Turn and baste the bird every 20 minutes and keep the foil on top throughout roasting. If the bird is not browned near the end of roasting, remove the foil. If the stock reduces quickly during roasting, add a little more. After 1$\frac{1}{2}$ hours loosen the string holding the legs to let heat reach the inside of the thigh.

To prepare mousse: make béchamel sauce and cool it. Work the ham twice through the fine blade of a grinder, then beat in the softened butter and the cold béchamel sauce. Whip the cream lightly and fold it into the ham mixture with the shredded tongue and truffle liquid; season well.

With a small sharp knife, cut away the suprêmes (all the breast meat of the turkey, down to the wing bone), leaving the wing bone attached to the carcass. Cut away the breast bone and ribs and discard them. Carve the suprêmes in thin slices.

Fill the body cavity with the mousse mixture, mounding it up well, and replace the suprêmes on the mousse, leaving an open space down the center. Arrange thin slices of truffle along the open space. Set the bird on a wire rack. Coat it all over with a little cool but still liquid aspic and chill until set.

Pour remaining aspic into a shallow tray, and chill until firm; then turn it out on dampened wax paper and chop it with a wet knife. Spread chopped aspic on a large platter and set the turkey on top. Fill each tartlet shell with cranberry sauce and arrange them around the turkey.

Note: the recipes in this menu serve 10–12 people.

Mound ham mousse mixture for turkey en gelée inside cavity of roasted bird to simulate the breastbone

Replace the suprêmes on mousse and arrange truffle slices down the center of bird

Accompaniment to entrée

Celery and Green Pepper Chartreuse

small bunch of celery, diced
2 green peppers, cored, seeded, cut in strips and blanched
2 slices of canned pimiento, drained and diced
2 envelopes gelatin
$\frac{1}{2}$ cup cold water
$1\frac{1}{2}$ cups boiling water
juice of 1 lemon
2 tablespoons onion juice
$1\frac{1}{2}$ cups mayonnaise
salt and pepper
2 bunches of watercress (for garnish)

2 ring molds (1$\frac{1}{2}$ quart capacity each)

Method
Lightly oil the ring molds.
Sprinkle gelatin over $\frac{1}{2}$ cup cold water and let stand 5 minutes until spongy. Pour boiling water over gelatin; stir until dissolved. Stir in lemon and onion juice and add enough cold water to make 4 cups. Let stand until cool, then stir over a bowl of ice water until it begins to thicken. At once beat vigorously until it looks foamy, then fold in mayonnaise, celery, peppers and pimiento. Season to taste, pour mixture into molds, cover with plastic wrap and refrigerate at least 2 hours or until firm.
A short time before serving, dip the molds quickly in and out of hot water and unmold the chartreuses onto platters. Garnish with watercress.

Have a basket of **assorted breads** on the buffet table — include small rolls, slices of French bread, Melba toast and assorted crisp crackers.
When guests have served themselves, serve Champagne or wine of your choice in glasses on a tray. Always offer a soft drink or water as alternatives for those who prefer it. Serve coffee at the end of the meal.

Fold the diced celery, green peppers and pimiento into the beaten gelatin and mayonnaise mixture

Garnish the center of the finished celery and green pepper chartreuse with a bunch of watercress

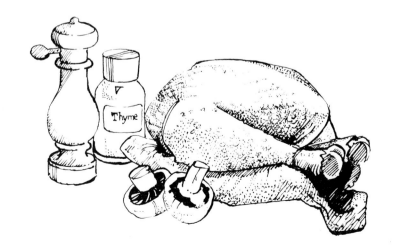

Dessert

Peach and Hazelnut Galette

8–10 fresh peaches or 1 large
   can (29 oz) sliced peaches
Chantilly cream (made with
   2 cups heavy cream, stiffly
   whipped and flavored with
   1 teaspoon vanilla and 6–8
   teaspoons sugar)
¾ cup confectioners' sugar
   (for sprinkling)
chocolate rounds, made with
   5 squares (5 oz) semisweet
   chocolate

For galettes
1½ cups flour
10 egg whites
1¾ cups sugar
1 cup shelled hazelnuts,
   browned and ground
1½ cups walnut pieces, ground
½ cup butter

Silicone paper

Makes 2 galettes.

Method
Draw 8 inch circles on 8
sheets of silicone paper. Set
the oven at moderate (350°F).
   To make galettes: sift the
flour. Beat the egg whites
until they hold a stiff peak
and fold in the sugar, prepared
nuts and flour. Cream the
butter, then warm it gently
in a small bowl until it will
pour but is not oily, and fold
into the galette mixture.
   Divide the mixture evenly
between the 8 sheets of
paper and spread it thinly in
8 inch rounds. Slide the
papers onto baking sheets
and bake in the heated oven,
1–2 at a time, for 20 minutes
or until pale golden brown.
Turn the baking sheets around
from time to time so the

rounds brown evenly.
   Transfer the rounds to a
wire rack, carefully peel off
the paper and cool. Bake the
remaining rounds in the same
way.
   If using fresh peaches, peel,
pit and cut them in thick
slices; if using canned peaches, drain them thoroughly.
Mix the peaches with the
Chantilly cream and chill well.
   A short time before serving,
sandwich the galette rounds
with the peach mixture, using
4 rounds for each galette.
Sprinkle the tops generously
with confectioners' sugar and
press the chocolate rounds
around the sides.

*Sandwich four of the galette
rounds with the peach and
Chantilly cream mixture.
Decorate with chocolate*

*To make chocolate rounds for galette, spread the melted
chocolate thinly and evenly on wax paper circles and refrigerate
them until hard*

To Brown and Grind Hazelnuts

Bake hazelnuts in a
moderately hot oven
(375°F) for 8–10 min-
utes. Then rub them
briskly in a rough cloth
to remove the dry skins.
Grind the hazelnuts in a
rotary cheese grater or
work a few at a time in a
blender.

To make Chocolate Rounds or Squares

For 24 rounds: grate or finely
chop 5 squares (5 oz) semisweet chocolate and melt on a
heatproof plate over a pan of
hot water, working with a
metal spatula until the chocolate is smooth; do not heat it
above tepid.
   Cut twenty-four 1½ inch
circles from wax paper. Spread
the chocolate thinly and evenly
on each circle; refrigerate until
hard (about 1 hour), then peel
away the wax paper.
   Alternatively, spread the
chocolate thinly and evenly on
wax paper or foil and, when it
is almost hard, cut out rounds
with a cookie cutter, or mark
into squares with a sharp knife.

Peach and hazelnut galette is sprinkled generously with confectioners' sugar, then decorated with chocolate rounds

The buffet luncheon for 24 includes (from left to right): strawberry gâteau, green salad, a platter of salmon steaks en chaudfroid with a tomato and shrimp garnish, orange mousse with lychees, salad Niçoise and more salmon steaks

WEDDING RECEPTIONS

Here are more suggestions for menus for wedding receptions. The buffet luncheon on the next page is particularly suited to a summer wedding because of the cold salmon entrée and the refreshing fruit desserts. The formal dinner (pages 18–21) includes a fillet of beef Wellington and the informal seated supper (pages 21–22) features chicken Khoreshe, made with eggplants, peppers and onions. The afternoon reception (pages 22–25) includes a mouth-watering coffee-flavored gâteau.

BUFFET LUNCHEON FOR 12

Salmon Steaks
en Chaudfroid

Salad Niçoise
Green Salad

Orange Mousse
with Lychees

Strawberry Gâteau

TIMETABLE

Day before
Poach salmon steaks and chill. Make aspic and chaudfroid sauce; coat salmon pieces with sauce and aspic and store, covered, in refrigerator. Chill and chop remaining aspic, store in wax paper in refrigerator.
Prepare tomatoes and vegetables for salad Niçoise and tomatoes for salmon garnish and store, covered, in refrigerator. Make vinaigrette dressing.
Wash salad greens and store in plastic bag in refrigerator.
Make orange mousses; store in molds, tightly wrapped, in refrigerator. Make cakes for gâteaux and store in airtight container.

Morning
Complete salmon en chaudfroid platter, add garnish and store, covered, in refrigerator.
Mix salad Niçoise with vinaigrette dressing, pile in salad bowl, cover and chill. Hull strawberries for gâteaux. Whip cream for mousses and make Chantilly cream for gâteaux. Unmold mousses, decorate and store in refrigerator. Complete strawberry gâteaux.

Just before serving
Mix green salad with vinaigrette dressing.
Arrange platters on table.

Note: recipe for vinaigrette dressing is given on page 63.

Salmon Steaks en Chaudfroid

24 salmon steaks (about $\frac{1}{2}$ lb each)
6 cups court bouillon

For chaudfroid sauce
2 tablespoons olive oil
2 shallots, finely chopped
$1\frac{1}{2}$ tablespoons paprika
$1\frac{1}{2}$ tablespoons tomato paste
3 cups mayonnaise
1 envelope gelatin
2 cups cool but still liquid aspic

For garnish
4 cups aspic
few sprigs of chervil or tarragon, or thin strips of cucumber peel
24 medium tomatoes, peeled, seeded (reserve juice from seeds for chaudfroid sauce) and cut in strips
2 lb cooked, peeled shrimps
$\frac{1}{2}$ cup vinaigrette dressing
2 teaspoons oregano or basil
salt and pepper

Method
Set oven at moderate (350°F). Pour hot court bouillon over the salmon steaks, cover with foil and poach them in the heated oven for about 20 minutes or until salmon flakes easily when tested with a fork. Let cool a little in the liquid, then remove steaks and discard skin and bones.

Divide each steak in half, tightly wrap each half in cheesecloth and press them between 2 baking sheets with a 2 lb weight on top until cold.

To make chaudfroid sauce: in a saucepan heat the oil, stir in shallot and cook for 3–4 minutes or until soft but not brown. Add paprika, tomato paste and the juice from the tomato seeds and cook, stirring, for 2–3 minutes. Strain and cool. Stir tomato and paprika mixture into the mayonnaise.

Unwrap salmon steaks and set them on a large wire rack with a tray underneath. Chill thoroughly.

Sprinkle gelatin over 2 cups of cool but still liquid aspic and let stand 5 minutes until soft. Heat the mixture gently, stirring until the gelatin is dissolved, and stir it into the mayonnaise. Cool the chaudfroid sauce, then stir over a bowl of ice water until it is on the point of setting. At once spoon over the salmon steaks to coat them.

To prepare garnish: decorate each chaudfroid-coated piece of salmon with a sprig of chervil or tarragon or a thin strip of cucumber peel dipped in aspic; chill. Stir the 4 cups aspic over a bowl of ice water until it is on the point of setting and spoon over the salmon steaks to coat them. and chill until firmly set. Pour the remaining aspic into a shallow dish and chill until set, then turn it out on dampened wax paper and chop it with a wet knife.

Mix the tomatoes and shrimps with vinaigrette dressing, herb and seasoning, cover and let marinate $\frac{1}{2}$–1 hour.

To serve, spread the chopped aspic in 1 or 2 large platters and arrange the salmon steaks on top in a fan shape. Pile the shrimp and tomato mixture in the center.

> **Chaudfroid** means literally 'hot-cold'. It is a cold dish of cooked fish, game or poultry that is coated first with a cold velouté or béchamel-based sauce (called a chaudfroid sauce) then with a layer of aspic.
> The variation here uses mayonnaise.

After poaching the salmon steaks, divide them in half and then discard skin and bones

Coat the salmon pieces with the chaudfroid sauce, cooled to the point of setting

Salad Niçoise

2 cucumbers, peeled, seeded and cut in strips
2 lb green beans, trimmed and cut diagonally into pieces
2 cups pitted ripe olives, drained
2 lb tomatoes, peeled, seeded and cut in strips
$\frac{3}{4}$ cup vinaigrette dressing
salt and pepper (optional)

Method

Lightly sprinkle cucumber strips with salt, let stand 30 minutes to draw out the juices (dégorger). Drain, rinse with cold water and pat dry with paper towels.

Cook green beans in boiling salted water for 8–10 minutes or until firm but tender; drain, refresh and drain again.

Combine vegetables with olives and tomatoes, mix with vinaigrette dressing and season to taste, if necessary. Pile in a serving bowl.

Orange Mousse with Lychees

1 can (6 oz) frozen orange juice, thawed
3 eggs
2 egg yolks
$\frac{1}{3}$ cup sugar
2 envelopes gelatin
$\frac{1}{2}$ cup water
$\frac{1}{2}$ cup heavy cream, whipped until it holds a soft shape

To finish

1 can (11 oz) lychees, drained
$\frac{1}{2}$ cup heavy cream, stiffly whipped
few shelled pistachios, or diamonds of angelica

Ring mold (1$\frac{1}{2}$ quart capacity); pastry bag and medium star tube

Method

Lightly oil the mold.

Put eggs, egg yolks and sugar in a bowl and beat until mixed. Set the bowl over a pan of hot but not boiling water and beat until the mixture is thick and light and leaves a ribbon trail when the beater is lifted. Take from heat and beat until cool. If using an electric beater, no heat is necessary. Sprinkle the gelatin over the orange juice mixed with $\frac{1}{2}$ cup water and let stand 5 minutes until spongy. Dissolve gelatin over a pan of hot water and stir into the egg mixture.

Chill bowl over a pan of ice water and stir gently until the mixture is on the point of setting. Fold in lightly whipped cream and pour at once into the prepared mold; cover and chill at least 2 hours or until set.

Shortly before serving, unmold the mousse onto a platter and fill the center with the lychees. Put the stiffly whipped cream into the pastry bag fitted with the star tube and decorate the top of the mousse with rosettes of whipped cream and pistachios or diamonds of angelica.

Strawberry Gâteau

$\frac{3}{4}$ cup flour
$\frac{1}{2}$ teaspoon ground cinnamon
pinch of salt
3 eggs
$\frac{1}{2}$ cup sugar
grated rind of $\frac{1}{2}$ lemon

To finish

1 quart strawberries, hulled
Chantilly cream (made with
  1 cup heavy cream, stiffly whipped and flavored with
  $\frac{1}{2}$ teaspoon vanilla and
  3–4 teaspoons sugar)

8 inch springform pan; pastry bag and medium star tube

Method

Set oven at moderately hot (375°F); grease the cake pan.

Sift flour with cinnamon and salt. Break the eggs into a bowl, gradually beat in the sugar and continue beating over a pan of hot water until the mixture is thick and leaves a ribbon trail when the beater is lifted. Take from the heat and continue beating until the mixture is cold. If using an electric beater, no heat is necessary.

Fold in the flour mixture and lemon rind and pour batter into the cake pan. Bake in heated oven for 20–25 minutes or until the cake springs back when the top is lightly pressed with a fingertip. Turn out onto a wire rack to cool.

To finish the gâteau: slice about one-quarter of the strawberries and mix with two-thirds of the Chantilly cream. Split the cake, sandwich halves with the cream and strawberry mixture and set gâteau on a platter.

Put remaining Chantilly cream into the pastry bag fitted with the star tube and decorate the gâteau with rosettes of cream. Arrange the remaining whole strawberries on top.

Quantities

The **orange mousse with lychees** and **strawberry gâteau** each serve 6 people so make 2 of each recipe to serve 24.

Do not attempt to double either recipe as such large quantities are hard to manage in a home kitchen.

FORMAL DINNER FOR 24

Pineapple Japonaise

Beef Wellington (hot or cold)

Ginger Soufflé

TIMETABLE

Two days before
Make pastry dough; chill.

Day before
For cold beef fillets, roast them and cool; make mushroom mixture, wrap fillets in dough and bake; cool and store covered.
Prepare ingredients and vinaigrette dressing for salad Niçoise; do not mix.
For hot fillets, roast and cool; make mushroom mixture, wrap fillets in dough; store, covered, in refrigerator.
Make sauce for beef, cover and store in refrigerator.
Prepare pineapple Japonaise; cover tightly and refrigerate. Make tarragon cream dressing, but do not add whipped cream.
Make soufflés and store, covered, in refrigerator.

Order of Work
6:00
If serving beef cold, set it on a platter, carve a few slices, garnish with watercress, cover and keep in refrigerator.
Mix ingredients for salad Niçoise and chill. If serving beef hot, prepare chosen vegetables.
Decorate tops of soufflés; store in refrigerator.
7:00
If serving beef hot, set oven at hot (425°F).
Complete the Japonaise.
Cook vegetables; keep warm.
7:30
Bake beef fillets.
7:50
Reheat sauce for beef and vegetables.
8:00
Serve dinner.

Pineapple Japonaise

4 fresh pineapples
$\frac{1}{2}$ cup sugar (or to taste)
juice of 1 lemon
5 cups tarragon cream dressing
$\frac{1}{4}-\frac{1}{2}$ cup light cream (optional)

Method
Leave the plume and skin on the pineapples and split them in half lengthwise. With a sharp knife cut out the cores and discard them. Cut out the flesh from each one in 1 piece with a grapefruit knife, cut in thin slices and return flesh to the pineapple shell. Sprinkle with sugar and lemon juice, cover and chill.

Before serving, coat the pineapples with tarragon cream dressing, thinned with a little light cream if it seems too thick.

Tarragon Cream Dressing

For about 5 cups: in a bowl or top of a double boiler beat 3 large eggs with a fork until mixed. Add $\frac{1}{2}$ cup sugar and gradually stir in $\frac{1}{2}$ cup tarragon vinegar. Stand the bowl over a pan of boiling water or heat the water in the bottom of double boiler and cook the mixture, stirring constantly, until it begins to thicken. Take the double boiler off the heat and continue stirring. When the mixture is thick, lift the container from the hot water and stir 1 minute longer. Season lightly and cool. Whip $1\frac{1}{2}$ cups heavy cream until it holds a soft shape and fold into the cool vinegar mixture. Taste for seasoning.

This dressing can be made, without adding the cream, in large quantities and stored in an airtight container in the refrigerator for up to 3 weeks. Add the whipped cream just before serving.

Beef Wellington

2 fillets of beef (5–6 lb each)
8 cup quantity of puff pastry
2 large thin sheets of pork
 fat (for barding) – optional
1 cup butter
salt and pepper
4 cups (1 lb) small mushrooms,
 sliced
2 tablespoons chopped parsley
2 teaspoons chopped mixed
 herbs (thyme, tarragon,
 basil)
1 egg, beaten to mix with
 1 teaspoon salt (for glaze)
bunch of watercress
 (for garnish)

Serve beef Wellington hot or cold, garnished with watercress. When served hot, serve a demi-glace sauce, or sauce Madère separately and vegetables of your choice. If served cold, serve with salad Niçoise (see page 17).

Method
Prepare the puff pastry dough, wrap it tightly and chill it overnight.
 Set oven at very hot (425°F). If the butcher has not already done so, trim the fillets, bard them with a thin layer of pork fat and tie securely with string to keep the shape. Brown the fillets on all sides in $\frac{3}{4}$ cup butter, sprinkle with salt and pepper, then roast them in the heated oven for 20 minutes. Take the fillets from the oven and let stand until cold. Discard the string and barding fat.
 In a skillet sauté mushrooms in the remaining butter until tender. Take from the heat, stir in the herbs and seasoning and let cool.
 Roll pastry dough out to a small rectangle, divide in two and roll each half to a large rectangle 10 inches wide and 4 inches longer than the fillets. Spread the cooled mushroom mixture along the center of each dough rectangle and set the fillets on top. Brush the dough edges with beaten egg, trim squares of excess dough from the corners and wrap up the beef like parcels, pressing the edges firmly so they stick together.
 Roll the fillets onto baking sheets, turning them so the dough seams are underneath. Brush tops with egg glaze and decorate with crescents or leaves (called fleurons) made from dough trimmings.
 Bake in a hot oven (425°F) for 30 minutes or until the pastry is browned and the meat is done (140°F on a meat thermometer for rare beef).

Puff Pastry

For 4-cup quantity
4 cups flour
2 cups butter
$\frac{1}{2}$ teaspoon of salt
2 teaspoons lemon juice
1–1$\frac{1}{2}$ cups ice water

Method
Reserve 2 tablespoons of butter and place the rest, lightly floured, between 2 pieces of wax paper. Pound with a rolling pin, remove the top piece of wax paper, fold the butter in half, replace the wax paper and pound again. Continue in this way until the butter is pliable but not sticky. Shape into a 5 inch square, dust lightly with flour and chill until firm but not hard.
 Sift flour and salt into a bowl or onto a marble slab and rub in the reserved butter. Add the lemon juice to 1 cup of the water. Make a well in the center of the flour and pour in the water and lemon juice. Mix with a spatula or round-bladed knife in the bowl or use your fingers on a marble slab. When a dough begins to form, add most of the remaining water. Mix to a firm, pliable dough, adding the remaining water if necessary.
 Lightly dust a marble slab or work surface with flour and knead the dough for 1–2 minutes. Roll out to a 12 inch square.
 Place the butter in the center of the dough and fold it over the butter, wrapping the sides and ends over like a parcel. Wrap in plastic wrap or a plastic bag and chill 15 minutes.
 Sprinkle the work surface lightly with flour, put down the dough with the joins facing up, and bring the rolling pin firmly down on the dough 3–4 times to flatten it slightly.
 Roll out to a rectangle about 5–6 inches wide and almost 3 times as long. Fold it into three, one end over the other, as accurately as possible; if necessary pull the corners to keep them in a rectangle. Seal the edges with the rolling pin and turn the dough half around to bring the open edges towards you. Roll out again and fold in three. Keep a note of the 'turns' made by marking the dough lightly with the appropriate number of fingerprints. Wrap and chill 15 minutes.
 Repeat this process, giving the dough 6 turns altogether with a 15 minute rest after every 2 turns. Wrap and refrigerate until needed.

Sauce Demi-glace

$\frac{1}{2}$ cup (2 oz) chopped
 mushrooms
1 tablespoon tomato paste
4 cups espagnole sauce
$\frac{1}{2}$ cup well-flavored stock
$\frac{1}{2}$ cup sherry
2 tablespoons butter

Makes 4 cups.

Method
Stir mushrooms into tomato paste and add both to the prepared espagnole sauce in a pan. Simmer 5 minutes, add the stock and continue to simmer uncovered, skimming often, until the sauce is well reduced.
 Add the sherry and beat in the butter. Do not boil after this, but reheat or keep warm in a water bath.

Sauce Madère

$\frac{1}{2}$ cup Madeira
1 tablespoon tomato paste
4 cups espagnole sauce
$\frac{1}{2}$ cup well-flavored stock
2 tablespoons butter

Makes 4 cups.

Method
Stir the tomato paste into the prepared espagnole sauce, simmer 5 minutes and add the stock. Continue to simmer, uncovered, skimming often, until the sauce is well reduced.
 Add the Madeira and beat in the butter. Do not boil after this, but keep warm or reheat when necessary in a water bath.

A recipe for Espagnole Sauce is given in Volume 2.

Ginger soufflé is decorated with rosettes of whipped cream and topped with thin slices of candied ginger

Ginger Soufflé

¾ cup finely sliced candied
  ginger
1 quart milk
8 eggs, separated
⅔ cup sugar
3 envelopes gelatin
¾ cup cold water
1½ cups heavy cream, whipped
  until it holds a soft shape

For decoration
1 cup heavy cream, stiffly
  whipped
few slices of candied ginger
few pistachios, finely chopped
  (optional)

*Soufflé dish (2 quart capacity);
  pastry bag; medium star tube*

This soufflé serves 12 people.
To serve 24, make it twice; do
not attempt to double the
recipe.

Method
Make a collar for soufflé dish
from a double layer of wax or
silicone paper and wrap it
around the dish so it extends
about 3 inches above the top
of dish; tie the collar with
string. Lightly oil inside of dish
and top part of collar.

If the ginger is at all dry,
pour boiling water over it, let
stand 15 minutes and drain
well before chopping.

Scald the milk. Put the egg
yolks and sugar in a bowl and
beat until thick and light. Stir
in the hot milk, return mixture
to the pan and heat gently,
stirring, until the custard
thickens slightly; do not let it
boil. Take from heat.

Sprinkle gelatin over the
water in a bowl and let stand
5 minutes until spongy. Add to
hot custard and stir until dissolved. Cover custard tightly
and let stand until cool.

Beat egg whites until they
hold stiff peaks. Add chopped
ginger to the cool custard and

chill over a pan of ice water,
stirring often, until it starts to
thicken. At once fold in the
whipped cream, then the
beaten egg whites. Pour
mixture into the prepared dish
and chill at least 2 hours or
until firmly set.

Just before serving, carefully peel off paper collar by
dipping a small metal spatula
into very hot water and running it between the 2 layers of
paper. Put the stiffly whipped
cream into the pastry bag
fitted with the star tube and
decorate the top of the
soufflé with rosettes of whipped cream; top them with the
candied ginger slices and
press finely chopped
pistachios around the edge of
the soufflé, if you like.

INFORMAL SEATED SUPPER FOR 24

Shellfish Louis

Chicken Khoreshe
Raisin Pilaf

Apricot Mousse Basque

TIMETABLE

Day before
Mix shellfish for salad and
prepare but do not add
celery and cucumber.
Cover tightly and refrigerate. Make mayonnaise
and dressing; store, covered, in refrigerator. Cook
chicken Khoreshe but do
not prepare or add egg-
plant; store, covered, in
refrigerator.
Cook raisin pilaf, cool,
cover and refrigerate.
Soak, cook and purée
apricots for mousses,
cover tightly and chill.
Make chocolate shapes.

Morning
Complete mousses, pile in
serving bowls and chill.

Order of Work
6:00
Decorate mousses with
chocolate shapes.
6:30
Slice eggplant for chick-
en, sprinkle with salt and
let stand 30 minutes to
draw out juices. Drain,
rinse, pat slices dry, fry
and arrange on chicken.
7:00
Set oven at moderate
(350°F).
7:15
Put chicken in oven to
bake, uncovered.
7:30
Put pilaf in oven to re-
heat.
Note: if using large casseroles for chicken Khoreshe or for rice, allow 15
minutes longer for cook-
ing and reheating.
Mix ingredients for shellfish salad, arrange on
plates. Garnish.
8:00
Serve supper.

Shellfish Louis

2 lb cooked lobster meat
3 lb cooked crab meat
3 lb cooked, peeled medium
  shrimps
1 cucumber, peeled, seeded,
  and diced
salt
2 cups diced celery
1 cup mayonnaise
1 cup vinaigrette dressing

For garnish
2 heads of Boston lettuce,
  washed and divided in leaves
2 boxes of cherry tomatoes
2 bunches of watercress

For Louis dressing
1½ cups mayonnaise
½ cup heavy cream
½ cup chili sauce
½ cup chopped green pepper
½ cup chopped scallions
¼ cup green olives, pitted and
  chopped
juice of ½ lemon (or to taste)

Method
Sprinkle cucumber with salt,
let stand 30 minutes to draw
out the juices (dégorger). Drain
and rinse with cold water and
pat dry.

Combine seafoods in a bowl
with celery and cucumber.

To make Louis dressing:
combine all ingredients in a
bowl and mix well; season to
taste with salt and lemon
juice. Chill.

In a separate bowl mix mayonnaise and vinaigrette dressing together. Pour dressing
over seafood mixture and mix
gently. Pile salad on lettuce
leaves on individual plates and
garnish with tomatoes and
watercress. Serve Louis dressing separately.

Note: recipe for vinaigrette
dressing is given on page 63.

Chicken Khoreshe

6 roasting chickens (3–3½ lb
   each), cut in pieces
5 large eggplants
salt and pepper
½ cup butter
10 large onions, sliced
5 green peppers, cored,
   seeded, cut in strips and
   blanched
5 lb tomatoes, peeled, seeded
   and sliced
grated rind of 2 lemons and
   juice of 5 lemons
1–1½ cups oil (for sautéing)
1 teaspoon saffron, soaked in
   ½ cup boiling water for
   30 minutes

If your casseroles are too
small, brown chicken pieces in
a skillet, then bake them in
layers with the vegetables in a
large roasting pan.

Method

Trim tops and bottoms from
eggplants but do not peel. Cut
in ¼ inch slices, sprinkle with
salt and let stand 30 minutes
to draw out the juices (dégorger). Drain, rinse and pat
them dry with paper towels.
Set oven at moderate (350°F).
   Divide butter between 2–3
large flameproof casseroles,
heat butter and brown chicken
pieces a few at a time on all
sides over medium heat.
Arrange pieces in the pots in
layers with vegetables; season
and add lemon rind and juice.
Cover and bake in heated oven
for about 1 hour.
   In a skillet heat the oil and
brown eggplant slices quickly
on both sides. Pour saffron
liquid over ingredients in the
pots and arrange eggplant,
overlapping, on top. Return
pots to the oven, uncovered,
and bake 15 minutes or until
the eggplant is browned and
chicken pieces are tender.
Serve hot with raisin pilaf.

Raisin Pilaf

5–5½ cups rice
3 cups raisins
¾ cup butter
3 onions, chopped
10–11 cups chicken stock
salt and pepper
3 cups browned, slivered
   almonds

*Large casserole (6 quart
capacity) or 2 smaller ones*

Method

Set oven at moderate (350°F).
   In a flameproof casserole
melt half the butter and cook
the onion until soft but not
browned. Stir in the rice and
cook, stirring, for 1–2 minutes
or until the grains look transparent; add 10 cups of the
stock, raisins, and seasoning.
   Bring the mixture to a boil,
cover and bake in heated oven
for 15 minutes. If the rice
looks dry, add more stock and
bake 5–7 minutes longer or.
until the rice is tender and
stock is absorbed. Let stand
10 minutes, then stir in the
almonds with a fork. Dot the
surface with remaining butter, cover and let stand in oven
for 5 minutes before serving
pilaf.

Apricot Mousse Basque

4 cups (½ lb) dried apricots
peeled rind and juice of
   2 lemons
½ cup sugar (or to taste)
10–12 egg whites
48 chocolate rounds or
   squares (see page 12)

This recipe serves 12 people
so make it twice to serve 24;
do not attempt to double it.

Method

Soak apricots if necessary
according to the package
directions. Cook them in the
soaking liquid or drain them,
then cover with water, add the
lemon rind and juice, and
simmer 15 minutes or until
very tender. Add sugar to
taste and cook 5–10 minutes
longer. Remove lemon rind,
work apricots through a sieve
or purée in a blender; let cool.
   Whip half the egg whites
until they hold a stiff peak,
add to half the apricot purée
a little at a time and continue
beating until mixture is stiff.
   Pile mousse into a serving
bowl and chill well. Repeat
with remaining egg whites
and apricot purée. Decorate
with chocolate rounds or
squares just before serving.

Note: dishes starred in the
menu are to be found by
referring to your Recipe Index.

AFTERNOON RECEPTION

★ *Selection of
Small Hot and Cold
Hors d'Oeuvre
and Pastries*
★ *Sausage Rolls
Assorted Sandwiches*

Almond Macaroons
★ *Petits Fours
Gâteau Moka
aux Amandes*

TIMETABLE

Day before
Prepare all savories and
hors d'oeuvre and keep
them in airtight contain-
ers. Make sandwiches and
store in plastic wrap in
refrigerator.
Make gâteaux moka and
butter cream frosting but
do not decorate. Store,
separately, in airtight
containers.
Make almond macaroons
and petits fours and store
in airtight containers.

Morning
Slice sandwiches and
arrange them with the
cold savories and hors
d'oeuvre on trays; cover
with plastic wrap and
store in refrigerator or in a
cool place.
Decorate gâteaux moka
and keep in cool place.
Arrange macaroons and
petits fours on trays and
keep covered.

Just before serving
Reheat hot hors d'oeuvre.

Canapés and Hors d'Oeuvre

Make a wide selection of small hot and cold savories. Any of the recipes for canapés and cocktail savories (Volume 7) and for hors d'oeuvre (see pages 116–125) are suitable for this afternoon wedding reception.

Savory Tartlets

Make individual quiches Lorraine, salés, smoked haddock and mushroom flans in small tartlet pans. The quantities for pastry and fillings given for these recipes in Volume 3 will each make 12–16 tartlets.

Suggestions for Sandwiches

Asparagus Rolls

Cut crusts from a small loaf of unsliced wholewheat bread. Spread the end with softened butter and cut off a thin slice. Place a cooked asparagus tip on the buttered side, sprinkle with finely chopped parsley and roll. Repeat with the rest of the loaf. Wrap rolls tightly in wax paper or plastic wrap and chill.

Ribbon Sandwiches

Cut a small, unsliced loaf of wholewheat bread in slices lengthwise; do not butter them. Make 4 different colored fillings: pink — chopped cooked ham, crisp bacon and pimiento bound with mayonnaise; yellow — hard-cooked egg yolks creamed with butter; white — cream cheese softened with cream; green — finely chopped watercress mixed with finely chopped pickle and mayonnaise. Spread the slices thinly with filling, season well and reshape into a loaf. Wrap in foil or a damp dish towel and chill for at least 3 hours. Cut into thin slices for serving.

Other suggestions for sandwiches are **smoked salmon roulades** (see Volume 7) and **coffee party sandwiches** (see Volume 13).

Asparagus tartlets, stuffed grapes (center) and smoked salmon roulades are ideal cocktail canapés for an afternoon reception (recipes are given in Volume 7)

Gâteau moka aux amandes is decorated with rosettes of coffee butter cream frosting

Gâteau Moka aux Amandes

¾ cup cake flour
pinch of salt
3 eggs
½ cup sugar

To finish
1 cup quantity butter cream
   frosting
1½—2 tablespoons dry instant
   coffee, dissolved in a little
   water
1 cup slivered almonds,
   browned
confectioners' sugar
   (for sprinkling)

*8 inch springform pan; pastry
   bag and medium star tube*

This recipe serves 6—8 people;
make it twice if you want to
serve more.

Method
Set oven at moderately hot
(375°F). Make the cake batter
as for strawberry gâteau (see
page 17) and bake in heated
oven for 20—25 minutes or
until the cake is golden
brown and springs back when
lightly pressed with a fingertip. Turn out onto a wire rack
to cool.

Make butter cream frosting
and flavor with coffee. Split
the cooled cake and sandwich
it with a thin layer of coffee
frosting.

Spread the top and sides of
the gâteau with more frosting,
reserving about one-quarter,
press the slivered almonds
all over the top and sides of
the cake and sprinkle with
confectioners' sugar. Put remaining frosting into the
pastry bag fitted with the star
tube and decorate the top
with rosettes of coffee frosting.

Coconut Macaroons

1½ cups shredded sweetened
   coconut
1 cup sugar
1½ tablespoons cake flour
½ teaspoon vanilla
2—3 egg whites (according to
   size)
few whole blanched almonds,
   split or glacé cherries,
   halved (to finish)

*Rice or silicone paper; pastry
   bag and ½ inch plain tube*

Makes 16 macaroons.

Method
Set oven at moderate (350°F).
   Combine shredded coconut,
sugar and cake flour in a bowl.
Add vanilla and enough egg
white to bind the mixture; beat
for about 5 minutes. Scrape
down the sides of the bowl and
let the mixture stand for 5
minutes.

If using rice paper, cut into
2 inch squares and place these,
shiny side down, on an ungreased baking sheet. If using
silicone paper, line a baking
sheet with it.

Beat coconut mixture for 5
minutes longer or until thick
and white. Using a pastry bag
fitted with the plain tube, pipe
coconut mixture into 2 inch
rounds onto rice or silicone
paper. Place a split almond or
halved cherry in center of each
macaroon and bake in heated
oven for 18—20 minutes or
until lightly browned.

Transfer macaroons to a
wire rack to cool. Tear away
edges only of rice paper or peel
macaroons from silicone paper
before they are cold.

Rice paper is an edible
paper made from rice
flour. It is obtainable from
oriental stores.

Butter Cream Frosting

For 1 cup: in a bowl beat 2 egg
yolks lightly until mixed. Dissolve ¼ cup sugar in ¼ cup
water, bring to a boil and boil
until the syrup spins a thread
when a little is lifted on a
spoon (230°F—234°F on a
sugar thermometer). Gradually pour hot syrup onto the
egg yolks, beating hard, and
continue beating until the mixture is cool and thick and light.
Cream 1 cup butter and beat it
into the egg and sugar mixture
with 2 teaspoons dissolved
instant coffee (or to taste), if
using.

Petits Fours

A selection of these little
pastries is ideal for wedding
receptions. Any of the recipes
in Volume 17 are suitable.

Coconut macaroons are simple cakes to make for an afternoon reception

Typical Mexican dishes are tacos (at back, left), tostadas (at front) and enchiladas, served with green and red sauces (recipes are on pages 31—32)

MEXICAN COOKING

In the days of the Aztecs, 400 years ago, cooking was considered an art in Mexico. With the influence of the Spanish Conquistadores and then the arrival in 1864 of Maximilian of Hapsburg as Emperor, his wife Carlotta and their sophisticated Court, this art was refined and skillfully blended to become the distinctive cuisine it is today.

Local ingredients have had a great influence on Mexican cooking. Chilies, sweet and mild, hot and pungent are used in profusion, along with tomatoes, both red and green. Beans in many colors — black, pink, speckled, pale yellow or dark brown — are an essential part of all Mexican meals.

Corn is equally vital — eaten fresh on the cob or dried and ground to make masa harina, Mexico's most important flour. No part of the ear is wasted, and even the husks are filled with chicken, meat or chilies to make tamales.

Lard is the principle cooking fat, with olive oil and salad oil next in order of preference; butter is seldom used.

Nuts and seeds, very finely ground, are favorite thickening agents and there are many kinds — peanuts, pecans, almonds, filberts, walnuts, pine nuts, sesame and pumpkin seeds.

The herbs and spices are similar to those familiar here: allspice, anise, bay leaf, cinnamon, cloves, cumin, oregano, saffron, mint and parsley. Coriander is indispensable, whether used fresh, when it is called cilantro (or sometimes Chinese parsley), or as dried seed that can be ground. Cilantro is available in Latin American and Chinese markets.

Chorizo, a hot Spanish sausage, is used frequently, as are garbanzo beans or chick-peas, available canned or dried. The plantain, a type of banana that needs cooking to make it edible, is popular and it can often be found in large city markets but, if not, regular bananas can be sub-stituted. Chocolate — or the potent tequila — are favorite drinks.

Traditional Mexican dishes are usually accompanied by, or cooked in, a sauce. This dates back to the time when chicken and other meat was so tough that it had to be cooked for a long time in soups and stews. Sauces are often based on chilies, onions and tomatoes, and may include nuts, sesame seed, garlic, herbs and spices and occasionally chocolate, all puréed together and then cooked. A blender makes puréeing easier; Aztec women used a crude stone mortar and pestle — a process that could take half a day, although results were excellent.

Styles of cooking in our Southwest and the states bordering on Mexico are very similar to the Mexican, not only because of the Spanish influence but also because the climate and crops — and consequently many ingredients — are the same.

The major difference is the use of meat in the Southwest. When the gold rush brought outsiders to the region, they started raising cattle and sheep and meat became plentiful. In Mexico meat is still a luxury for most people. Poultry has always been the staple instead of meat, and turkeys were domesticated by the Aztec Indians long before the Spanish came to Mexico. The areas along the coast are filled with fish — lobsters, giant shrimps and turtle, codfish, red snapper and abalone.

As in Madrid, the dinner hour in Mexico City is very late. Generally, however, the main meal throughout Mexico is in the afternoon. One reason is the common belief that eating a large meal at night in high altitude areas is bad for the digestion.

The following dishes all use ingredients that are available in large supermarkets or in Spanish, Mexican and Puerto Rican neighborhood stores.

PEPPERS AND CHILIES

The variety of Capsicum peppers, a genus that includes chilies, sweet bell peppers and pimientos, is enormous — there are about 90 species. They are not related to the true pepper — peppercorns are the dried berries of the Piper nigrum plant.

Chilies are vital to Mexican cooking and more than 60 varieties are grown. Most are red, and these are often dried and ground to powder (although the heart-shaped red pimiento and the red bell pepper are never dried). Green chilies are usually hotter than red ones and they are available fresh in some parts of the country and are widely sold in cans. Green sweet bell peppers are available all year in many markets. Red bell peppers (ripe green peppers) are usually sold only at certain times of year. Pimientos do not keep well and are usually sold only in cans.

Types of Pepper and Chili

Ancho is the all-purpose red chili. Full-flavored and mildly pungent, it is the only dried chili that keeps well all year.

Mulato chilies, larger and darker than anchos and very pungent, are almost always used dried.

Pasilla, a very dark red and thin dried chili, is even more pungent than the mulato.

Mirasol colorados are mild red peppers much lighter in color than mulatos or anchos.

Serrano, small and relatively mild in taste, is an all-purpose green chili that is sold both fresh and canned.

Poblano, another green chili, comes either hot or mild and is sold both fresh and canned.

Jalapeño, a pointed hot green chili is sold fresh and canned.

Bell — red bell peppers are green ones left to ripen completely; both are mild and used fresh.

Hontaka chilies are very pungent and often used in making cayenne, crushed red pepper and other packaged hot red peppers.

Cayenne, a thin long pepper — green or red — is always hot. It is usually dried and powdered to make cayenne pepper and is now cultivated in most of the warm parts of the world.

Tabasco, a tiny pungent bright red pepper, is also used to make Tabasco sauce to flavor soups, and piquant or cocktail sauces.

To Prepare Peppers and Chilies

Dried chilies: wash in cold water, remove veins, stems and seeds and cut chilies into small pieces. Pour on about 6 cups boiling water per cup of chilies and add 2 teaspoons vinegar. Let soak for about 30 minutes.

Fresh chilies: soak in cold salted water for 1 hour to remove some of the hot taste.

In some recipes fresh chilies and bell peppers must be peeled before use or blanched in boiling water, drained and refreshed.

To peel fresh chilies and bell peppers: hold each one over a flame with a fork, or roast them in a hot oven (400°F) until blistered all over. Wrap in damp paper towels and let rest for about 30 minutes. Peel off the skin, split in half and trim away seeds and core. **Watchpoint:** the oils in the flesh of fresh hot chilies can burn your skin. It is best to wear rubber gloves.

Canned chilies and pimientos: rinse in cold water and drain, reserving liquid if necessary.

Shown below are: **1** *bell pepper;* **2–7** *a variety of chilies —* **2** *large cayenne;* **3** *serrano;*
4 *mulato;* **5** *serrano;* **6** *hontaka;* **7** *jalapeño;* **8** *ancho and* **9** *mirasol colorados*

1 *Place dough on press between sheets of wax paper*

2 *Press down hard so that the tortilla dough is flattened*

3 *Very carefully pull wax paper away from the dough*

4 *Fry tortillas until golden and stack them between paper towels*

ing the dough does not hurt it.

Cook on an ungreased griddle or skillet over moderate heat for about 2 minutes on each side or until the edges begin to curl and the tortillas are lightly browned.

Keep tortillas warm by wrapping them separately in paper towels, then in a hot, damp napkin and putting in a low oven.

Tortillas

Tortillas are a Mexican staple. They are thin flat pancakes made with masa harina. Before serving they can be baked in the oven or heated in a skillet until lightly browned; or they may be fried until crisp. They are eaten plain or served with a sauce; or they are stuffed or topped with a savory filling.

Tortilla Press
A special press is used to flatten the dough simply and very fast. Place a ball of dough the size of a walnut between 2 sheets of wax paper on the press and close firmly. Peel off the wax paper and use the tortilla as directed in the recipe.

The ancient Aztec method was to take the ball of dough between wet hands and pat it out to a 6–8 inch circle just under one-eighth inch thick.

Corn Tortillas

2 cups masa harina (corn flour)
1 teaspoon salt
1¼–1⅓ cups lukewarm water

Griddle or skillet; tortilla press (optional)

Makes 12 tortillas.

Method
Mix the masa harina with the

salt in a bowl with enough water to form a soft dough.

Divide dough into balls the size of a walnut and flatten in a tortilla press or with a rolling pin between 2 sheets of wax paper until they are very thin and about 6 inches in diameter.

Watchpoint: if they stick, the dough is too soft. Add more masa harina and work dough so it is no longer sticky. Work-

Wheat Flour Tortillas

2 cups all-purpose flour
1 teaspoon salt
¼ cup lard or shortening
½ cup lukewarm water

Griddle or skillet; tortilla press (optional)

In parts of Mexico, mainly in the North, wheat flour tortillas are popular. They were first made by the Spanish who came to Mexico and cooked their own foods, using Indian methods.

These tortillas are delicious hot with butter and salt or spread with guacamole (see page 37) and rolled. They can also be spread with the meat filling for tamales (see page 34), then rolled. Makes about 12 tortillas.

Method
Sift the flour with the salt into a bowl. Rub in the lard or shortening with the fingertips until the mixture resembles crumbs. Add enough water to make a stiff dough.

Divide the dough into balls the size of walnuts and flatten in a tortilla press or roll on a lightly floured board until they are as thin as possible.

Cook on a lightly greased griddle or skillet over moderate heat. The secret of a soft tortilla – one that is to be filled and rolled up – is to cook it about 15 seconds on one side, then turn it immediately and cook about 2 minutes on other side. Return to original side for another minute or until golden spots appear.

Queso y Chile
(Cheese and Chili)

Dice $\frac{1}{2}$ lb Monterey Jack or American Muenster cheese and mix it with 1 cup green sauce (see page 39).

Serve as a filling for tortillas or quesadillas (see page 33).

Huevos Rancheros
(Country-style Eggs)

8 small tortillas
8 eggs
2 tablespoons lard or oil
$\frac{1}{4}$ cup butter
1 small onion, finely chopped
1 clove of garlic, crushed
salt and pepper
refried beans (see page 37)
$1\frac{1}{2}$ cups tomato sauce
(see page 40)

Method
Heat the lard or oil in a skillet and fry the tortillas until limp or crisp, according to taste. Drain on paper towels and arrange 2 of them side by side on each plate. Keep warm.

Melt the butter in the skillet, add the onion and garlic and fry until soft. Drop in the eggs and fry until just set. Season with salt and pepper and put an egg on each tortilla. Spoon some of the tomato sauce over each egg and pile the fried beans on the side of each plate. Serve the eggs on tortillas with remaining sauce.

Tostadas

Tostadas are crisply fried tortillas. They are served with a mixture of fish, chicken and meat or with a sauce poured over them, then garnished with shredded lettuce, radishes and olives. Tostadas must be assembled at the last minute so they stay crisp.

Tostadas de Pescado
(Fish Tostadas)

12 tortillas
2 cups cooked flaked fish
1 medium onion, finely chopped
$3\frac{1}{2}$ tablespoons oil
2 tomatoes, peeled, seeded and chopped
$\frac{1}{2}$ teaspoon oregano
salt
black pepper, freshly ground
4–6 tablespoons grated Parmesan cheese
$\frac{1}{2}$ head of lettuce, shredded
green sauce (for serving) – see page 39

Method
Cook the onion in 2 tablespoons oil until soft. Stir in the tomatoes and oregano, continue cooking until the mixture is thick. Stir in the fish, season to taste and heat thoroughly.

In another skillet fry the tortillas in remaining $1\frac{1}{2}$ tablespoons hot oil until crisp and brown on both sides. Drain on paper towels.

Cover the tortillas with some of the hot fish mixture, sprinkle each one with a little Parmesan cheese, then add a layer of shredded lettuce, sprinkled with salt and pepper. Serve green sauce in a separate bowl.

Tostadas con Chorizo
(Tostadas with Sausage)

12 tortillas
4 chorizo sausages
3 tablespoons oil
$1\frac{1}{2}$ cups refried beans (see page 37)
$\frac{1}{2}$ head of lettuce, shredded
salt
2 teaspoons vinegar
1 medium onion, finely chopped
$1\frac{1}{2}$ cups guacamole (see page 37)
3–4 tablespoons grated Parmesan cheese

Method
Remove the skins from the sausages, chop them finely and fry them in 1 tablespoon oil over medium heat, stirring frequently, until browned. Heat the beans.

Fry the tortillas in $1\frac{1}{2}$ tablespoons hot oil over moderate heat until crisp and brown on both sides. Drain on paper towels and keep warm. Spread the hot beans on the tortillas, cover them with a layer of the sausage, pile on a layer of lettuce seasoned with a little salt, the vinegar and remaining oil, sprinkle the onion on top, then add a layer of guacamole and finish with a little Parmesan cheese on each tostada. Serve at once.

Tostadas de Gallina
(Chicken Tostadas)

12 tortillas
2 cups cooked chicken, chopped
3 tablespoons oil
2 scallions, finely chopped
3–4 ripe tomatoes, peeled, seeded and chopped
salt and pepper
1 avocado, peeled, seeded and thinly sliced
$\frac{1}{2}$ head of lettuce, shredded
1 teaspoon oil
1 teaspoon vinegar
12–16 ripe olives, pitted and sliced

Method
Fry the tortillas in $1\frac{1}{2}$ tablespoons of hot oil until crisp and brown on both sides. Drain on paper towels and keep warm.

Cook scallions in the remaining $1\frac{1}{2}$ tablespoons oil until soft. Stir in tomatoes and cook, stirring frequently, until they form a thick sauce. Stir in the chopped chicken and salt and pepper; simmer about 10 minutes and taste for seasoning.

Cover the tostadas with the hot chicken mixture and top with a layer of avocado slices. Garnish with shredded lettuce sprinkled with a little oil and vinegar and slices of ripe olives.

Tacos

A taco is a dish made with small tortillas – about 4 inches in diameter – in fact, what most Americans think of as a Mexican sandwich. The tortillas may be baked so they can be spread with filling and folded in half or they can be fried until crisp in lard or oil and served with chilies on the side and sauces like green or red sauce (see pages 39 and 40) or guacamole (page 37).

Tacos de Queso
(Cheese Tacos)

12 small tortillas
2 fresh (or canned) poblano or serrano chilies
3 tomatoes, peeled, seeded and chopped
1 scallion, finely chopped
salt
black pepper, freshly ground
pinch of sugar
3½ tablespoons oil
¼ lb sliced Monterey Jack or American Muenster cheese, cut in squares

For a milder flavor, green bell peppers may be substituted for the chilies.

Method
Prepare the chilies and, if fresh, peel and core them.

Work the chilies, tomatoes and scallion together in a mortar and pestle or in a blender until smooth. Season and add sugar to taste. Heat 2 tablespoons oil, stir in the chili mixture and cook, stirring, over a moderate heat for 5 minutes; keep warm.

Fry the tortillas until crisp in remaining oil. Put a piece of cheese and a spoonful of purée on each tortilla and serve at once.

Tacos en Cazuela
(Tacos Casserole with Beef)

12 small tortillas
1 lb lean ground beef
¼ cup oil
1 onion, finely chopped
1 red or green bell pepper
4–5 tomatoes, peeled, seeded and finely chopped
2–3 anchovy fillets, chopped
2 tablespoons raisins
2 tablespoons red wine
1 tablespoon chopped walnuts
¾ cup beef stock
1 teaspoon oregano
salt and pepper
½ cup grated Monterey Jack or American Muenster cheese

These tacos are stuffed, rolled and fastened with a toothpick, then baked in a casserole with sauce.

Method
Prepare the bell pepper, core, seed and finely chop it. Set oven at moderately hot (375°F).

Heat the oil and fry the ground beef until it is lightly browned, stirring constantly. Stir in half of the onion, pepper, tomatoes, all of the anchovy, raisins, wine and walnuts. Cook over a low heat for 5 minutes, stirring frequently.

In a saucepan combine the remaining onion, bell pepper and tomatoes with the stock and oregano. Season to taste with salt and pepper and simmer for about 15 minutes.

Heat the tortillas in a low oven to soften them. Put some of the beef mixture on each tortilla, roll up and fasten with a toothpick. Place them in an oiled baking dish or casserole. If any meat mixture is left over, shape it into little balls and put in the casserole with the rolled tortillas.

Pour the sauce over the top and sprinkle with the grated cheese. Bake in heated oven for 18–20 minutes or until the cheese is melted and brown.

Enchiladas

Enchiladas are tortillas that are dipped in sauce before frying, then rolled around a filling and covered with remaining sauce before baking in the oven.

Enchiladas Verdes
(Green Enchiladas)

24 small tortillas
6 fresh or canned poblano chilies or 6 green bell peppers
1 can (10 oz) Mexican green tomatoes
1 teaspoon ground coriander
salt
black pepper, freshly ground
1 teaspoon sugar (or to taste)
3 tablespoons lard or oil
2 cups cooked diced lean pork
1 onion, finely chopped
¼ cup grated Parmesan cheese

For garnish
shredded lettuce
chopped radishes
chopped onion

Method
Prepare the chilies or bell peppers and, if fresh, peel and core them, then cook in boiling, salted water for about 5 minutes; drain. Canned ones do not need cooking.

Drain green tomatoes, reserving liquid, and purée a little at a time in a blender with chilies or green peppers, coriander, and enough of the reserved tomato liquid to make a smooth purée. Alternatively, pound the green tomatoes, chilies or green peppers and coriander in a mortar and pestle and add enough of the reserved tomato liquid to make a smooth purée. Season this sauce with salt, pepper and sugar to taste and set aside.

In a skillet heat the lard or oil. Dip the tortillas, one at a time, into the sauce and fry for 10–15 seconds on each side until they soften and go limp. Combine the diced pork and finely chopped onion and season to taste with salt and pepper.

Spread a little of the mixture on each tortilla, roll them up and place on a greased baking dish; heat in a moderate oven (350°F) for 10 minutes.

Reheat the sauce and pour over the tortillas. Sprinkle with grated Parmesan cheese and serve hot with a garnish of shredded lettuce, chopped radishes and chopped onion.

Enchiladas con Carne
(Meat Enchiladas)

24 small tortillas
1 lb ground beef
6 dried ancho chilies, reserving soaking water
3 ripe tomatoes, peeled, seeded and chopped
2 onions, finely chopped
1 clove of garlic, chopped
¼ cup oil
salt
black pepper, freshly ground
3 tablespoons lard or oil (for frying)
¼ teaspoon sugar (or to taste)
½ cup grated Parmesan cheese
chopped lettuce, radishes, olives (for garnish) – optional

Method
Prepare the chilies. Combine them and their soaking water

Serve red or green sauce with tostadas (at front), tacos or enchiladas – all made with tortillas (recipes on pages 30–31)

Quesadillas

Quesadillas are little turnovers. They can be made from tortilla dough or a special dough made with masa harina and a flavoring such as chili.

The turnovers are filled with a variety of stuffings, then fried until hot and golden. Quesadillas, 4 inches in diameter, can be served as a first course or they can be made about 2 inches in diameter for cocktails.

Masa de Quesadilla con Queso
(Cheese dough for Quesadillas)

2 cups masa harina
$\frac{1}{4}$ cup grated Parmesan cheese
$\frac{1}{2}$ teaspoon baking powder
$\frac{1}{2}$ teaspoon salt
1 tablespoon oil
$\frac{1}{2}-\frac{3}{4}$ cup lukewarm water
lard or oil (for frying)

Makes 12 regular quesadillas or 24 small ones.

Method
In a bowl mix the masa harina, grated cheese, baking powder and salt together. Stir in the oil and enough lukewarm water to make a stiff but workable dough.

Shape dough into tortillas (see page 30), spread with a filling, fold over and pinch the edges with fingertips to seal.

Fry the quesadillas in plenty of hot lard or oil on both sides until golden. Drain on paper towels and serve hot.

Masa de Quesadilla con Chile Ancho
(Chili dough for Quesadillas)

2 cups masa harina
2 dried ancho chilies, reserving soaking water
$\frac{1}{2}$ teaspoon salt
4–6 tablespoons lukewarm water
lard or oil (for frying)

Makes 12 regular quesadillas or 24 small ones.

Method
Prepare the chilies. Drain and chop them finely.

Mix the masa harina with salt, stir in chilies and add their water with enough lukewarm water to make a stiff but workable dough.

Shape dough into tortillas (see page 30), and continue as for previous recipe, browning on both sides.

Relleno de Papas
(Potato filling for Quesadillas)

2 medium potatoes, peeled, diced, boiled until tender and drained
1 onion, finely chopped
$\frac{1}{2}$ green bell pepper
1 clove of garlic, peeled and chopped
salt
black pepper, freshly ground

Add leftover stew or gravy to mixture, if you like. Makes enough for 12 quesadillas.

Method
Prepare the green pepper. Core, seed, chop and blanch it. Mix potatoes with onion, green pepper and garlic; season to taste.

with the tomatoes, the chopped onion and garlic and purée a little at a time in a blender. Alternatively, pound the drained chillies, tomatoes, half the chopped onion and garlic in the mortar and pestle and then stir in the soaking water from the chilies.

In the skillet heat 2 tablespoons oil, stir in the chili purée and cook over medium heat for 5 minutes, stirring frequently. Add salt, pepper and sugar to taste, and reserve.

Sauté the ground beef in remaining 2 tablespoons oil until brown. Drain off all fat, mix meat with a little of reserved sauce to bind mixture and stir in 3–4 tablespoons grated Parmesan cheese.

In a skillet heat 3 tablespoons lard or oil and dip the tortillas, one at a time, into the reserved sauce. Fry on each side for 10–15 seconds or until tortilla is soft. Put a little of the beef mixture on each tortilla, roll up and place in a greased baking dish. Cover with remaining sauce. Sprinkle the top with remaining cheese and bake in a moderate oven (350°F) for 18–20 minutes or until heated through. Garnish with the chopped lettuce, radishes and olives, if you like.

Picadillo
(Mexican Meat Hash)

1 lb chopped lean beef
2 tablespoons oil
1 onion, finely chopped
2 cloves of garlic, chopped
2 ripe tomatoes, peeled, seeded and chopped
1 fresh or canned jalapeño chili
$\frac{1}{4}$ cup raisins
2 tablespoons coarsely chopped stuffed olives
pinch of ground cinnamon
pinch of ground cloves
pinch of ground cumin
salt
black pepper, freshly ground
$\frac{1}{2}$ cup peanuts or slivered almonds

This recipe is very popular in Mexico. Makes enough filling for 12 quesadillas or 24 tamales. Double the quantities to serve as a main course for 4 people.

Method
Prepare the chili and, if fresh, peel, core and slice it; if canned, seed and slice it.

Heat oil in a skillet, add beef and fry, stirring frequently, until browned. Stir in onion and garlic and continue cooking for 5 minutes.

Add remaining ingredients except nuts and cook over a low heat, uncovered, for 20–25 minutes, stirring occasionally, until picadillo is thick. Before serving, add nuts and taste for seasoning.

Tamales

The dough for tamales is made with masa harina. It is usually spread on a corn husk and filled with a variety of meats and sauces. The tamales are then rolled, tied at both ends and steamed. Refried beans, picadillo, pieces of cheese wrapped in strips of peeled green chili, pickled vegetables of all kinds and meat make excellent fillings for tamales.

Corn husks are available at Mexican specialty stores. If you cannot find them, substitute the silicone paper that is used for lining baking sheets.

Basic Tamal Dough

2 cups masa harina
$\frac{1}{3}$ cup lard
$1\frac{1}{2}$ teaspoons baking powder
$1\frac{1}{2}$ teaspoons salt
about $1\frac{1}{2}$ cups lukewarm stock
24 dried corn husks

Makes about 24 tamales.

Method
Soak corn husks in hot water for about 1 hour or until softened. Pat them dry with paper towels.

To make dough: work the lard until soft and light. Sift the masa harina, baking powder and salt and mix with the lard. Add enough of the warm stock to make a soft, spreadable dough and beat 5 minutes or until the dough is very light.

To finish tamales: place about 2 tablespoons of tamal dough on each husk and spread it to the sides, leaving room at top and bottom so the ends can be folded over or tied. Put a tablespoon of chosen filling in center of the dough and fold over sides so filling is completely covered by dough. Fold or tie ends and put tamales on a rack in a steamer over boiling water. Cover and steam for 45 minutes to 1 hour or until the dough is firm.

Serve in the husk, so guests can open their own tamales and discard the corn husks.

Relleno de Jamón y Chile
(Ham and Chili Filling for Tamales)

1 cup chopped cooked ham
1–2 fresh or canned serrano or jalapeño chilies
1 small onion, chopped
1 package (3 oz) cream cheese
2 ripe tomatoes, peeled, seeded, and chopped
salt (optional)

Makes enough for 24 tamales.

Method
Prepare the chilies and, if fresh, peel and core them. Seed and chop chilies and mix with all remaining ingredients. Taste and add salt if needed.

Use as directed in basic tamal dough recipe.

Relleno de Carne
(Meat Filling for Tamales)

2 lb boneless lean beef or pork, cut into 2 inch cubes
1 onion, stuck with 3–4 cloves
2 cups chili sauce (see page 40)
2 tablespoons oil
salt
black pepper, freshly ground

Makes enough for 24 tamales.

Method
Simmer the meat and the onion stuck with cloves, covered, in enough salted water to cover for about $1\frac{1}{2}$–2 hours or until very tender, skimming from time to time. Drain stock and reserve it. Discard onion and pull meat into shreds.

Stir $\frac{1}{2}$ cup meat stock into the chili sauce. Heat the oil in a skillet, add the sauce and cook for about 5 minutes, stirring constantly.

Add the meat and cook over a low heat, uncovered, for about 30 minutes, adding more stock if needed; the filling should be very thick. Taste for seasoning. Finish as directed in basic tamal dough recipe.

Tamal de Cazuela con Pollo
(Tamal Chicken Pie)

$3\frac{1}{2}$–4 lb chicken
$1\frac{1}{2}$–2 quarts chicken stock

For filling
6 dried poblano chilies
1 large onion, chopped
2 cloves of garlic, chopped
3 tomatoes, peeled, seeded
    and chopped
2 tablespoons oil
salt
black pepper, freshly ground
$\frac{1}{2}$ cup grated Parmesan cheese

For tamal dough
3 cups masa harina
$\frac{1}{2}$ cup lard
2 teaspoons baking powder
2 teaspoons salt
1–$1\frac{1}{2}$ cups chicken stock (from
    cooking chicken)

Casserole (2 quart capacity)

Method
Prepare the chilies.
    Put whole chicken in a kettle with enough stock to cover and bring to a boil. Cover, reduce heat; simmer chicken $\frac{3}{4}$–1 hour or until tender when tested with a fork. Let stand until chicken is cool enough to handle, then drain, reserving liquid; remove all meat from bones, discarding skin and fat; cut into chunks and reserve.
    Mix chilies, onion, garlic and tomatoes; work mixture a little at a time in a blender with enough water from chilies to make a coarse purée. Alternatively, finely chop chilies, onion, garlic and tomatoes; moisten with a little chili water.
    Heat oil in a skillet, add purée and cook gently about 5 minutes, stirring constantly. Season to taste, and set aside.
    Make tamal dough, as for

basic dough on page 34. Set oven at moderate (350°F).
    Grease the casserole and line bottom and about two-thirds up sides with dough. Arrange chicken pieces in the center, add about half the sauce, sprinkle with cheese and cover with remaining dough. Bake in heated oven for about 1 hour or until tamal is firm. Heat remaining sauce and serve separately with the pie.

OTHER MEXICAN DISHES

Menudo
(Tripe Soup)

$2\frac{1}{2}$ lb honeycomb tripe
1 cow's foot, split (optional)
$2\frac{1}{2}$ quarts water
1 large onion, finely chopped
2 cloves of garlic
1 teaspoon oregano
$1\frac{1}{2}$ cups hominy
salt and pepper

For serving
2 scallions, chopped
2 tablespoons chopped fresh
    coriander
1 lemon, cut in wedges
red sauce (see page 40)

This soup is always served on New Year's Day for breakfast.

Method
If using cow's foot: scrub it thoroughly, cover with water; simmer, covered, about 1 hour.
    Trim the tripe, wash thoroughly and soak overnight in cold water, then blanch in salted water for 15 minutes

and drain. Cut into 1 inch squares and add to $2\frac{1}{2}$ quarts water. Add onion, garlic, cow's foot, if used, oregano, hominy and seasoning. Simmer about 6 hours or until tripe is very tender adding more water if pan gets dry. Serve in bowls, sprinkled with chopped scallions and coriander. Serve lemon wedges and red sauce separately.

Mexican Seviche

1 lb fillets of very fresh
    pompano, mackerel or sole
juice of 6 limes or 5 lemons
2 ripe tomatoes, peeled,
    seeded and chopped
1 onion, finely chopped
2 fresh or canned jalapeño
    chilies
$\frac{1}{4}$ cup oil
1 tablespoon dry white wine
$\frac{1}{4}$ cup finely chopped parsley
1 teaspoon oregano
salt
black pepper, freshly ground

For garnish
1 avocado, peeled, seeded and
    sliced
$\frac{1}{4}$ cup pitted ripe olives

Seviche is made with fish that is 'cooked' by marinating in lime or lemon juice. Versions of it are found all along the coasts of Latin America. The Mexican seviche is usually spiced with chili and flavored with tomatoes and herbs. Seviche can be made with almost any firm-fleshed fish such as flounder, pompano, whitefish and haddock. For a luxury dish, bay or sea scallops make a superb seviche.

Method
Prepare the chilies and, if fresh, peel, core and chop them.

Cut the fish into small squares or into thin strips. Put into a deep enamel or ceramic dish and cover with the lime or lemon juice. Cover and let marinate in the refrigerator for 6–8 hours, turning fish after 3 hours. When fish is marinated, drain and reserve the liquid.
    Mix the tomatoes, onion, chilies, oil, white wine, parsley and oregano with salt and pepper. Pour in one-third cup of the reserved liquid and toss carefully with the fish. Chill thoroughly before serving. Garnish with slices of avocado and the ripe olives.

Torte de Elote
(Corn Casserole)

5 ears of corn, shucked
4 eggs, separated
½ cup melted butter
1 teaspoon sugar
salt and pepper

*Baking dish or soufflé dish
(5 cup capacity)*

Method
Butter the dish and set the oven at hot (400°F).

Cut the corn from the cob and work the grains in a blender or through the fine blade of a meat grinder. Beat the egg yolks to mix them. Combine the corn with the melted butter, sugar, egg yolks and season to taste.

Beat the egg whites until they hold a stiff peak and fold them into the corn mixture.

Pour at once into the prepared dish and bake in heated oven for 20–25 minutes or until puffed and brown. Serve at once with yoli sauce (see page 40).

Calabacitas con Jitomate
(Zucchini with Tomatoes)

1 lb zucchini, trimmed and cut into ½ inch slices
4 tomatoes, peeled, seeded and chopped (reserving the juice)
3 tablespoons oil
1 onion, finely chopped
1 clove of garlic, crushed
2 canned jalapeño chilies, drained, seeded and cut into strips
salt
black pepper, freshly ground

Method
Heat the oil in a flameproof casserole. Add the onion and cook until soft but not brown. Add the zucchini, tomatoes, garlic, chilies and seasoning to taste.

Add the strained juice from the tomatoes, then cover the pot and cook over very low heat, stirring occasionally, for 30 minutes or until the zucchini are tender; serve hot.

Garbanzos con Pimientos
(Chick-peas with Pimientos)

2 cups (1 lb) dried garbanzos (chick-peas)
1 can (4 oz) pimientos, cut into strips, with their liquid
1 onion, finely chopped
2 tablespoons oil
2 cloves of garlic, chopped
black pepper, freshly ground
1½ quarts water
2 cups (1 lb) canned tomatoes, chopped
salt

Method
Soak garbanzos overnight in water to cover. Drain, add onion, oil, garlic and pepper and 1½ quarts water. Cover, bring to a boil and simmer 1 hour.

Stir in tomatoes and salt and cook 1–1½ hours longer or until garbanzos are tender. Stir pimientos into bean mixture, heat thoroughly, taste for seasoning and serve.

Ejotes con Chiles
(Green Beans with Chilies)

1 lb green beans
2 fresh or canned serrano or poblano chilies
3 tablespoons oil
1 onion, finely chopped
salt
black pepper, freshly ground
1 teaspoon sugar

Method
Prepare the chilies and, if fresh, peel and core them. Chop chilies.

Trim the green beans and snap them in half. Cook in plenty of boiling salted water for 8–10 minutes or until they are just tender. Drain, refresh, drain again and set aside.

In a skillet heat the oil and fry the onion until soft. Stir in the beans and chopped chilies, season and add sugar. Heat, shaking the skillet frequently, until the beans are very hot.

Chiles Rellenos
(Stuffed Chilies)

8 fresh or canned poblano chilies
¾ lb Monterey Jack cheese, cut in 3 X 2 inch pieces
3 eggs, beaten with ½ cup milk
salt and pepper
1 teaspoon oregano

Stuffed chilies are an excellent accompaniment for any meat dish.

Method
Prepare the chilies and, if fresh, peel and core them.

Place chilies in a shallow ovenproof dish and insert a piece of cheese in each one. Cover with the egg mixture and sprinkle salt, pepper and oregano on top.

Bake in a moderate oven (350°F) for 25 minutes or until the eggs are set.
Note: a Mediterranean version of cheese-stuffed peppers was given in Volume 5, and a recipe for stuffed peppers with a choice of beef, corn or mushroom stuffing was included in Volume 4.

Frijoles
(Beans)

2 cups (1 lb) dried pinto or red kidney beans
1½ quarts water
black pepper, freshly ground
salt
¼ cup lard or oil

Serves 6 people.

Method
Soak beans overnight in water to cover. Drain, rinse and put them in a saucepan with 1½ quarts water and pepper. Cover, bring to a boil, then reduce the heat and simmer the beans for 1–2 hours, depending on the type of bean, or until they are tender and most of the liquid is absorbed. Add salt halfway through cooking.

Pour the beans into a large roasting pan and mash them thoroughly with a fork.

Heat the lard or oil in a large skillet, add the beans, season to taste, mix to make a smooth, heavy paste and cook, stirring frequently, until all the liquid has evaporated and the beans are hot.

Frijoles Refritos
(Refried Beans)

Prepare beans as for frijoles recipe. In a large skillet heat 2 tablespoons lard. Add the mashed beans, little by little, stirring thoroughly. Cook 10–15 minutes over low heat, stirring constantly, until the beans are smooth, stiff and dry. Add more lard from time to time as the beans cook, if you like.

Ensalada de Aguacate
(Avocado Salad)

1 large avocado, seed removed and sliced
3 fresh or canned poblano chilies, peeled, seeded and cut into strips
3 tomatoes, peeled, seeded and cut into strips
4 large Boston lettuce leaves
3 tablespoons olive oil
1 tablespoon lime juice
salt and pepper

Method
Mix the chilies and tomato strips together. Arrange the lettuce leaves on a platter or on 4 individual plates and surround with slices of avocado. Beat the olive oil into the lime juice and season to taste. Pour the dressing over the chili and tomato mixture and over the avocado slices.

SAUCES

In Mexico sauces play an important role in cooking, as they do in France. Chilies, tomatoes, avocados, herbs and seasonings are combined to produce a colorful variety of sauces, ranging from bland through hot to fiery.

Mole is a sauce made with chilies and cooked in fat so as to blend the flavor of chilies with the other ingredients. The best known one is mole Poblano, made with chilies and chocolate.

Some sauces are an integral part of a specific dish; others are made and served separately.

Guacamole
(Avocado Sauce)

2 large ripe avocados
1 small canned serrano or jalapeño chili, drained and chopped
2 tablespoons lime or lemon juice
1 tablespoon finely chopped onion
pinch of sugar
1 ripe tomato, peeled, seeded and chopped
1 teaspoon salt
black pepper, freshly ground

Serve guacamole (avocado sauce) as a dip with fried tacos

This can be used as a sauce for cooked or raw vegetables such as tomatoes, cauliflower, green beans or carrots. It is popular as a dip with fried tacos or tortillas and can be served as a salad, garnished with thinly-sliced onions and radishes. Makes about 2 cups.

Method
Halve the avocados, remove seeds, peel off the skin and mash. Add all ingredients except tomato and mash together with a fork. Stir in the chopped tomato, season to taste. If sauce is not to be used immediately, cover securely with plastic wrap and refrigerate.

Ingredients for turkey mole 1 include both ancho and pasilla chilies, a square of chocolate, peanuts, almonds, sesame seed, cloves, tomatoes and onions

Mole Poblano 1
(Turkey Mole 1)

10–12 lb turkey
10 dried mulato chilies
10 dried pasilla chilies
6 dried ancho chilies
2–3 quarts chicken stock or
   salted water
4–6 tablespoons lard
$\frac{1}{3}$ cup whole blanched almonds,
   browned
$\frac{1}{3}$ cup shelled peanuts, browned
1 tortilla, coarsely chopped
2 tablespoons sesame seed
$\frac{1}{4}$ teaspoon ground cloves
$\frac{1}{4}$ teaspoon ground cinnamon
$\frac{1}{2}$ teaspoon aniseed
3 ripe tomatoes, peeled,
   seeded and chopped
1 onion, finely chopped
1 square (1 oz) unsweetened
   chocolate, cut in pieces
salt
black pepper, freshly ground
1 teaspoon sugar
2 tablespoons sesame seed
   (for garnish)

Serves 8–10 people.

Method
Prepare the chilies.

Cut the turkey into 8 pieces; put into a large kettle, add enough chicken stock or salted water to cover and bring to a boil. Cook, covered, for 1 hour. Drain thoroughly, reserving the stock.

Heat 4 tablespoons lard in a large skillet, brown the turkey pieces and transfer them to a large flameproof casserole; reserve the lard.

Work the almonds, peanuts, tortilla, 2 tablespoons sesame seed, cloves, cinnamon, aniseed, tomatoes, onion, and chilies in a blender to make a coarse purée. Alternatively, pound the almonds, peanuts, tortilla, sesame seed and aniseed in a mortar and pestle. Stir in the tomatoes, cloves, cinnamon, onion and chilies and work through a food mill to make a coarse purée.

Heat the lard remaining in the skillet, if necessary adding a little more, add the purée and cook for about 5 minutes, stirring constantly.

Add 2 cups of the reserved stock, the chocolate pieces, salt and pepper to taste and sugar. Heat, stirring constantly, until the chocolate melts. Pour the sauce over the turkey in the casserole, cover and cook over a low heat or in a moderately low oven (325°F) for about 1 hour or until turkey is tender when tested with a fork. Be sure the sauce does not stick to the bottom of the pan.

The turkey should be very tender and the sauce should be the consistency of heavy cream. If sauce is too thick, stir in a little of the reserved stock. Just before serving, sprinkle the turkey with sesame seed.

Turkey Mole 2

Cut a 5 lb turkey into serving pieces and simmer them, covered, in a casserole with chicken stock to cover for 30 minutes or until almost tender when tested with a fork. Drain, thin green mole sauce with a little of the stock and pour over the turkey.

Cover and cook over very low heat for 15–20 minutes or until the turkey is tender. Do not let the sauce boil.
Serves 4–6 people.

Chicken Mole

Cut two $2\frac{1}{2}$–3 lb chickens into serving pieces and prepare as for turkey mole 2.
Serves 4–6 people.

Pork Mole

Cut $2\frac{1}{2}$ lb boneless loin of pork into 2 inch cubes and cook as for turkey mole 2, simmering it $1\frac{1}{2}$ hours or until tender before adding mole sauce.
Serves 4–6 people.

Mole Verde
(Green Mole)

8 fresh or canned poblano
   chilies
$\frac{1}{2}$ cup pepitas (squash seed)
$\frac{1}{2}$ cup chopped walnuts
$\frac{1}{2}$ cup whole blanched almonds,
   slivered
1 large onion, chopped
1 clove of garlic, chopped
2 cans (10 oz each) green
   tomatoes
$\frac{1}{2}$ cup chopped fresh coriander
   or 1 teaspoon coriander seed
salt
black pepper, freshly ground
2 tablespoons oil
$\frac{1}{4}$–$\frac{1}{2}$ cup stock

Pepitas are grown in Mexico where they are roasted and eaten like peanuts or shelled to use in dishes. They are available in Mexican and Spanish specialty markets. Makes about 6 cups.

Method
Prepare the chilies and, if fresh, peel and core them.

Work the pepitas in a blender, $\frac{1}{4}$ cup at a time, until they are as fine as possible; reserve them.

Mix walnuts, almonds, onion, garlic, green tomatoes and their liquid, coriander and the chilies and work them in a blender to a coarse purée. Add the ground pepitas with salt and pepper to taste.

Heat the oil in a skillet, add the sauce and cook for 5 minutes, stirring. Thin the sauce with enough stock to make it the consistency of heavy cream; taste for seasoning. Serve with chicken, pork loin or tenderloin or with a small turkey.

Salsa Verde
(Green Sauce)

1 can (10 oz) green tomatoes,
   drained and chopped
1 onion, chopped
2 fresh or canned serrano or
   jalapeño chilies
1 green bell pepper
1 tablespoon chopped fresh
   coriander or $\frac{1}{2}$ teaspoon
   ground coriander, mixed
   with 1 tablespoon chopped
   parsley
salt
black pepper, freshly ground

This sauce is good with tongue, chicken and fish. Makes about 1 cup. (An Italian green sauce was given in Volume 5.)

Method
Prepare the chilies and, if fresh, peel and core them. Core and seed bell pepper, then chop chilies and pepper.

Combine all ingredients in a blender and work until the sauce is quite smooth. Alternatively, mash ingredients together with a fork and work through a food mill. Season to taste.

Salsa Roja
(Red Sauce)

2 large ripe tomatoes, peeled, seeded and finely chopped
2 fresh or canned cayenne or hot red chilies
1 onion, finely chopped
1 tablespoon chopped parsley
1 tablespoon chopped fresh coriander or $\frac{1}{2}$ teaspoon ground coriander
pinch of ground cloves
salt
black pepper, freshly ground
pinch of sugar

Serve this all-purpose sauce cold with meats, fish, poultry, fried eggs or as filling for tacos and tostados. Makes 3 cups.

Method
Prepare the chilies and, if fresh, discard seeds. Chop chilies finely.

Combine all the ingredients, mix well and season to taste.

Salsa Yoli
(Yoli Sauce)

3 tomatoes, peeled, seeded and finely chopped
2 green bell peppers
salt
1 tablespoon oil
$\frac{1}{2}$ cup dry cottage cheese
$\frac{1}{2}$ cup sour cream

Serve this sauce with tostados and tacos. Makes 4 cups.

Method
Prepare the bell peppers, core and seed them, then work in a blender or through the finest blade of a meat grinder. Mix peppers with tomatoes and add salt to taste. In a skillet heat the oil and fry mixture over high heat 1 minute; cool. Add cheese and sour cream and mix well.

Salsa de Perejil
(Parsley Sauce)

$\frac{3}{4}$ cup finely chopped parsley
$\frac{1}{4}$ cup whole blanched almonds, finely chopped
3 tablespoons wine vinegar
$\frac{1}{3}$ cup olive oil
salt
black pepper, freshly ground

Serve with meat or fish on sliced tomatoes, vegetable salad and with cooked or un-cooked cauliflower. Makes about 1$\frac{1}{4}$ cups.

Method
Combine ingredients in a bowl, season to taste and mix well.

Salsa de Jitomate
(Tomato Sauce)

2 large ripe tomatoes, peeled, seeded and chopped
2 tablespoons oil
1 onion, finely chopped
1 clove of garlic, finely chopped
$\frac{1}{2}$ teaspoon sugar
salt
black pepper, freshly ground
1 tablespoon chopped fresh coriander or $\frac{1}{2}$ teaspoon ground coriander

Serve this sauce hot or cold. Makes about 1$\frac{1}{2}$ cups.

Method
Heat the oil in a skillet, add onion and garlic and fry until soft but not brown. Stir in tomatoes and cook over a low heat for 15 minutes, stirring often. Add sugar, salt and pepper to taste. Stir in coriander and cook a few minutes longer.

Salsa de Pimientos
(Pimiento Sauce)

4 slices of canned pimiento, drained
4 hard-cooked eggs
1 cup heavy cream
salt
black pepper, freshly ground
8–10 pimiento-stuffed olives, thinly sliced
1 tablespoon lime or lemon juice

Serve on cold poached fish, with fish salad, with hard-cooked eggs or with cold chicken. Makes about 2 cups.

Method
Halve the eggs, scoop out the yolks and finely chop the whites. Work the pimiento, egg yolks, cream and salt and pepper (to taste) in a blender, or alternatively work the pimiento and egg yolks through a food mill and stir in the cream with seasoning. Stir in the sliced olives, chopped egg whites and the lime or lemon juice.

Salsa de Chile
(Chili sauce)

3 dried mulato chilies
3 dried pasilla chilies
2 ripe tomatoes, peeled, seeded and chopped
1 large onion, chopped
1 clove of garlic, chopped
2 tablespoons oil
1 tablespoon parsley, chopped
1 teaspoon oregano
salt
black pepper, freshly ground
$\frac{1}{2}$ teaspoon sugar
1 tablespoon wine vinegar

A mild chili sauce for meats and tortillas. Makes about 2 cups.

Method
Prepare the chilies and drain them. Work chilies, tomatoes, onion and garlic to a purée in a blender or food mill. Heat the oil in a skillet, add the purée and cook, stirring constantly, for about 5 minutes. Stir in the parsley, oregano, salt, pepper and sugar. Let the sauce cool. Add the vinegar and stir thoroughly. Taste for seasoning.

DESSERTS

Budin de Mango
(Mango Pudding)

2 ripe mangoes
½ cup whole blanched almonds, ground
4 egg yolks, beaten to mix
½ cup sugar
½ cup sherry
¼ teaspoon cinnamon
6 large macaroons, crumbled
½ cup apricot jam
½ cup heavy cream, whipped until it holds a soft shape
¼ cup browned, slivered almonds

Glass bowl (1½–2 quart capacity)

Method
Peel mangoes, remove pits and finely chop the flesh.

Mix mangoes, ground almonds, egg yolks, sugar, half the sherry and cinnamon in a saucepan. Cook the mixture over low heat, stirring constantly, until it thickens.
Watchpoint: do not let the mixture boil. Take from the heat and let cool.

Arrange half the crushed macaroons in a glass serving bowl, sprinkle with some of the sherry, spread them with apricot jam and cover with half the mango mixture.

Add another layer of macaroons, remaining sherry and rest of mango mixture. Cover the top with whipped cream; sprinkle with slivered almonds.

Capirotada
(Bread Pudding)

5 slices of buttered white bread, crusts removed
1 cup water
1½ cups dark brown sugar
2 eggs, separated
1 tablespoon butter, softened
¼ cup cognac
1 banana, sliced
1 tart apple, peeled, cored and sliced
2 tablespoons raisins
½ cup shelled peanuts
¼ lb Monterey Jack cheese, sliced
½ teaspoon cinnamon

Method
To make the syrup: put the water with the sugar in a small saucepan, heat gently until sugar dissolves, then bring to a boil and boil steadily for 5 minutes (220°F on a sugar thermometer).

Beat the egg whites until they hold a stiff peak. Beat the butter, egg yolks and cognac together. Gradually beat in the hot syrup and fold in the egg whites.

Butter a large shallow baking dish and arrange a layer of buttered bread in it. Then add a layer of banana, apple, raisins and peanuts and cover with cheese. Continue layering until the dish is almost full, ending with a layer of bread. Sprinkle each layer with cinnamon.

Pour the syrup and egg mixture over it and bake in a moderately low oven (325°F) for 25–30 minutes or until the pudding is set.

Pan de Muerto
(Bread of the Dead)

4–4½ cups flour
1 package dry or 1 cake compressed yeast
½ cup lukewarm water
1 teaspoon aniseed
1 teaspoon salt
½ cup sugar
½ cup butter, melted
6 eggs, beaten to mix
1 tablespoon orange flower water or 1 teaspoon orange extract
grated rind of 1 orange

To finish
1 cup confectioners' sugar
2–4 tablespoons hot milk or water
pink sugar crystals (for sprinkling)

Method
Sprinkle the yeast over the lukewarm water and let stand 5 minutes or until dissolved. Stir in about 1 cup of the flour or enough to make a light, spongy dough and work into a ball. Place in a bowl, cover with a damp cloth and let stand in a warm place or until doubled in bulk.

Crush aniseed in a mortar and pestle. Sift remaining flour, salt and sugar into a bowl. Work in melted and cooled butter, eggs, orange flower water or extract, crushed aniseed, and grated orange rind. Knead mixture on a floured board until smooth. Work in yeast dough and continue kneading 5 minutes or until dough is very smooth and elastic. Sprinkle with additional flour when needed. Cover with a damp cloth and let stand in a warm place for about 1½ hours or until doubled in bulk.

Shape into 2 round loaves, reserving a little dough for decorations. Set oven at moderately hot (375°F).

Set loaves on a greased baking sheet and attach pieces of dough rolled between the palms of your hands to make 'cross-bones'. Cover with a damp cloth and let stand in a warm place for 20 minutes or until almost doubled in bulk.

Bake loaves in heated oven for 30 minutes or until bread sounds hollow when tapped on the bottom. Cool on a wire rack.

To finish: mix the confectioners' sugar with enough hot milk or water to make a thin icing. Brush the loaves with icing and sprinkle with sugar crystals.

Dia de los Muertos
(Day of the Dead)

The Mexican equivalent of All Souls' Day, November 2, is the day when the people of Mexico visit and tend their family graves. However, it is not a day of mourning – the Day of the Dead is a joyful fiesta. Everyone carries flowers, especially orange marigolds, the flower of the dead. They eat candy skulls and skeletons, and also a special sweet yeast bread Pan de Muerto, flavored with orange rind, orange flower water and aniseed and decorated with pieces of baked dough shaped like cross-bones, and topped with sugar crystals.

Cocado, coconut pudding, is flavored with cinnamon and served cold, decorated with whipped cream and almonds

Cocado
(Coconut Pudding)

1 cup shredded coconut
1 cup sugar
1 cup water
pinch of salt
4 cups milk
2 sticks of cinnamon
3 egg yolks, beaten to mix
½ cup heavy cream, whipped
   until it holds a stiff peak
¼ cup browned, slivered
   almonds

*Glass bowl (1 quart capacity);
pastry bag and large star
tube (optional)*

Method

Butter the glass bowl.

Put the sugar and water in a saucepan and boil steadily until syrup spins a thread when a little is lifted on a spoon and tested between the finger and thumb (230°F—234°F on a sugar thermometer).

Add coconut and salt and cook, stirring constantly, until coconut absorbs sugar syrup and looks dry.

Scald 3½ cups of milk with cinnamon, cover and let stand 15 minutes to infuse. Strain, add coconut mixture; stir constantly over low heat until thoroughly mixed.

Stir the remaining milk into the egg yolks, stir in a little of the coconut mixture, then add it gradually to the remaining coconut mixture in the pan. Cook over a low heat, stirring constantly, until the mixture thickens; do not let it boil. Cool slightly. Pour into the buttered bowl and refrigerate.

When the cocado is cold, cover the top with whipped cream or put cream into pastry bag fitted with a star tube and pipe rosettes on the top of the cocado. Decorate with slivered almonds and serve.

MEXICAN DRINKS

Chocolate Mexicano

Chocolate originated in Mexico and when the Spaniards conquered that country in 1519 they found that the Emperor Montezuma and his Court consumed 50 large jars of drinking chocolate a day. Sugar was not known; the drink was flavored with vanilla and spices and taken cold. For over a century the Spaniards managed to keep from the rest of Europe, the secret of how chocolate beans were prepared; eventually the secret leaked out and it became a favorite drink all over the world.

Mexicans like chocolate so much that they have even invented a cup and saucer called a 'mancerina' to hold in church. Then they can continue to enjoy their chocolate while listening to lengthy sermons.

Mexican chocolate comes in round pieces that are marked in quarters and it is flavored with cinnamon; regular sweet chocolate with a little ground cinnamon can be used instead.

The chocolate drink is whisked with a molinillo — a foot-long wooden beater with a grooved bulb at the end. The bulb is set in the liquid with the long handle between the palms of the hands. When the hands move back and forth quickly, the bulb rotates and beats the chocolate until it is light and foamy. A hand or electric beater can be substituted.

To make Mexican Chocolate

For each cup of chocolate add 1 oz Mexican chocolate to 1 cup milk and beat with a molinillo over low heat until the chocolate melts and the mixture is foamy. If using regular sweet chocolate, add a pinch of ground cinnamon to the saucepan. Pour into a cup and serve at once.

Tequila

Besides the popular hot chocolate drink, Mexicans love to drink tequila — a potent liquor made from the agave plant. The traditional way to take tequila is to lick a little salt from the crook between thumb and finger of the hand, take a drink of tequila with the other hand, then suck a wedge of lime.

Délices de sole au Parmesan are garnished with fried bananas and shredded almonds (recipe is on page 46)

Choose from two appetizers — délices de sole au Parmesan or tomato and Gruyère toasts. Follow with an entrée of little squabs bonne femme simmered in a sauce with onions and potatoes, then finish with liqueur-flavored orange soufflé or coffee Bavarois as dessert.

This is a menu where one wine will suit both appetizers and the entrée. The dry white wines of the upper Loire, most notably Pouilly-Fumé and Sancerre, have a charming bouquet and a crisp flavor that goes well with fish and poultry and makes a happy change from the dry white wines of Burgundy. California vintners are now using the same sauvignon blanc grapes to produce comparable wines sold under the grape name or occasionally labeled Fumé Blanc.

BANANAS WITH SOLE MAKE A PLEASING PAIR

Délices de Sole au Parmesan
or
Tomato & Gruyère Toasts

Squabs Bonne Femme
Green Beans with Pine Nuts
or
Buttered Zucchini

Orange Soufflé Nantaise
or
Coffee Bavarois

White wine — Sancerre (Loire)
or Dry Sauvignon Blanc (California)

TIMETABLE

Day before
Cook bacon and blanch onions for squabs bonne femme.
Make chicken stock.
Make breadcrumbs and mix with cheese for the sole.
Clarify butter for frying sole.

Morning
Season and truss squabs and keep in refrigerator.
Peel potatoes and keep in cold, salted water.
Cut bread for tomato and Gruyère toasts; peel and slice tomatoes.
Make the orange soufflé and keep in refrigerator *or make Bavarois and keep tightly covered in refrigerator; make Suchard sauce and store in an airtight container.*

Assemble ingredients for final cooking from 6:30 for dinner around 8 p.m.

> You will find that **cooking times** given in the individual recipes for these dishes have sometimes been adapted in the timetable to help you when cooking and serving this menu as a party meal.

Order of Work
6:30
Decorate soufflé and keep in refrigerator.
6:45
Unmold Bavarois and decorate.
Set oven at moderate (350°F) if using.
Start browning potatoes and squabs.
7:00
Put squabs in oven or cook on top of stove.
Coat fish with flour, egg and breadcrumb mixture *or soak bread for toasts.*
Fry toasts, complete and leave ready for broiling.
Start cooking green beans *or zucchini.*
7:30
Remove squabs and potatoes to a deep dish and keep warm; turn oven to low.
Brown onions and bacon, make sauce, add to squabs and potatoes and keep hot in oven.
7:45
Drain and refresh green beans.
Fry sole and keep warm; fry bananas and garnish fish; keep hot.
Broil cheese and tomato toasts.
Toss green beans in butter; transfer beans *or complete zucchini and transfer* to serving dish and keep hot.
8:00
Serve appetizer.

Appetizer

Délices de Sole au Parmesan

1½ lb fillets of sole
2 tablespoons seasoned flour (made with pinch of salt and pinch of pepper)
1 egg, beaten to mix
¼ cup fresh white breadcrumbs
2 tablespoons grated Parmesan cheese
6 tablespoons clarified butter

For garnish
2 small bananas, peeled and cut in thick diagonal slices
1 tablespoon butter
¼ cup shredded almonds
squeeze of lemon juice

Method
Cut the fish fillets into wide diagonal strips and pat them dry with paper towels. Toss them with the seasoned flour and coat with beaten egg. Mix the breadcrumbs and grated cheese together and toss the pieces of fish in the crumbs until well coated.

In a skillet heat the clarified butter and fry the fish over fairly high heat until golden brown, turning constantly. Pile them on a hot platter (without draining) and keep warm.

To prepare the garnish: wipe out the frying pan with paper towels. Heat the tablespoon of butter in the pan until it foams, add the banana slices and fry quickly, turning them until brown. Add the almonds and brown them also. Squeeze in the lemon juice, at once spoon bananas and almonds around the fish fillets and serve very hot.

Cut the fillets of sole into thick diagonal strips, then coat the strips in the breadcrumb and cheese mixture

To garnish the sole, fry the banana slices in foaming butter until brown, then brown the shredded almonds

Alternative appetizer

Tomato and Gruyère Toasts

2 tomatoes, peeled, seeded
 and thickly sliced
2 slices of Gruyère cheese,
 cut in four
1 egg, beaten to mix
¾ cup milk
salt and pepper
4 slices of white bread
¼ cup butter
1 teaspoon Dijon-style mustard
little sugar
½ teaspoon rosemary leaves
1 tablespoon butter (to finish)

Method

Mix the egg, milk, salt and pepper together. Trim crusts from the bread, cut each slice in half and coat with the egg mixture.

Heat the butter in a frying pan and fry the slices of bread slowly so that a crust forms on the bottom, then turn the bread and brown it on the other side.

Spread a thin layer of mustard on the fried bread and place the slices of cheese on top. Put in a shallow baking dish ready for broiling.

Arrange the sliced tomatoes on top of the cheese, sprinkle lightly with salt, pepper, sugar and a few leaves of rosemary. Put a few slivers of butter on each tomato slice and broil until the cheese bubbles and begins to brown. Serve hot.

◀ For tomato and Gruyère toasts, fry the pieces of bread (soaked in egg mixture) in butter until they are golden brown

Top the toasts with a slice of ▶ cheese and tomato before broiling and put a few slivers of butter on each tomato slice

Tomato and Gruyère toasts are sprinkled with rosemary and broiled until the cheese begins to brown

Squabs bonne femme are served with the sauce and garnish spooned over them and sprinkled with chopped parsley

Entrée

Squabs Bonne Femme

4 squabs
$\frac{1}{4}$ lb piece of bacon
salt and pepper
$\frac{1}{4}$ cup butter
12—16 small new potatoes,
 peeled
1 cup chicken stock
bouquet garni
10—12 small white onions,
 blanched and peeled
2 teaspoons arrowroot (mixed
 to a paste with 2 tablespoons
 light cream)
1 tablespoon chopped parsley

Trussing needle and string

Rock Cornish game hens are a more economical alternative to squabs in this recipe.

Method

Simmer the bacon in water in a covered pan for 45 minutes, then cut into lardons ($\frac{3}{4}$ X $\frac{1}{4}$ X $\frac{1}{4}$ inch pieces).

Season the cavities of the squabs and truss them securely. Melt 3 tablespoons of the butter in a large flame-proof casserole, add the potatoes and brown them, shaking the pan so they brown evenly. Take them out, add the squabs and brown on all sides. Moisten with $\frac{1}{4}$ cup of the stock, add the bouquet garni, cover tightly and cook over low heat or in a moderate oven (350°F) for 15 minutes. Add the potatoes and continue cooking 15—20 minutes or until the squabs and potatoes are tender.

Take the squabs from the pan, discard the trussing strings, put the birds in a deep dish and keep warm. Remove potatoes from the pan with a

Add the browned potatoes to squabs halfway through cooking

slotted spoon and keep them warm with the squabs. Discard the bouquet garni.

Melt the remaining table-spoon of butter in the pan. Add the bacon and onions; cover and cook, shaking the pan occasionally, until they are brown and tender. Pour in the remaining stock and bring to a boil, scraping to remove any sediment from the pan sides. Stir the arrowroot paste into the sauce and cook, stirring, until thickened; taste for seasoning.

Spoon the sauce, the bacon and onions over squabs and potatoes or return squabs and potatoes to the sauce in the pan. Sprinkle with parsley before serving with green beans with pine nuts or buttered zucchini.

Accompaniment to entrée

Green Beans with Pine Nuts

1 lb green beans
$\frac{1}{2}$ cup pine nuts
2 tablespoons butter
1 tablespoon chopped parsley
salt and pepper

Method

Trim the beans and leave them whole, if they are small, or halve them if they are large. Cook them in boiling salted water for 10—15 minutes or until just tender, drain, refresh and drain again.

Melt the butter, add the beans and pine nuts; cook over medium heat, tossing the beans carefully, until very hot and well coated with butter. Add the parsley and seasoning and pile in a hot serving dish.

Alternative accompaniment to entrée

Buttered Zucchini

4—8 small zucchini
2—3 tablespoons butter
1 tablespoon water
salt and pepper
2 teaspoons chopped parsley
2 teaspoons chopped mixed
 herbs — basil, tarragon,
 thyme (optional)

Do not peel the zucchini, but wipe them with a damp cloth and trim the stem and flower end. They are at their best when only 4—5 inches long and can be cooked whole. If larger, they should be cut into diagonal slices.

Method

If large, blanch the zucchini in boiling salted water for 5 minutes, drain and refresh under cold running water.

Put them in a heavy-based pan with the butter and water; season, press a piece of buttered foil or brown paper on top (this retains all the moisture) and put on the lid. Cook over very low heat for 15—20 minutes or until the zucchini are very tender but still keep their shape. Sprinkle with chopped herbs and serve.

Dessert

Orange Soufflé Nantaise

2 large macaroons, crushed
2 tablespoons Grand Marnier, Triple Sec, Curaçao or other orange liqueur
3 large eggs, separated
¾ cup sugar
grated rind and juice of 3 small oranges
grated rind of 1 lemon
juice of ½ lemon with enough water added to make ¼ cup
1 envelope gelatin
1 cup heavy cream, whipped until it holds a soft shape

For decoration
½ cup heavy cream, stiffly whipped and sweetened with 1 tablespoon sugar
2 large macaroons, crushed
3–4 tiny macaroons (optional)

Soufflé dish (3 cup capacity)

Method
Tie a double thickness of wax paper around soufflé dish to make a collar and lightly oil paper. Soak half the crushed macaroons in liqueur.

In a heatproof bowl mix egg yolks, sugar, orange and lemon rinds and orange juice. Set bowl over a pan of simmering water and beat until mixture is light and thick enough to leave a ribbon trail on itself. Take from heat and continue beating until cool. If using an electric beater, no heat is needed. Put lemon juice and water into a small pan, sprinkle gelatin over and let stand 5 minutes until spongy. Dissolve gelatin over a pan of hot water and stir into orange mousse mixture. Chill mixture, stirring frequently over a pan of ice water. Beat egg whites until they hold a stiff peak.

When orange mixture is cool and starts to set, at once fold in lightly whipped cream, followed by the egg whites. Pour mixture into prepared soufflé dish, layering it with soaked macaroon crumbs and ending with a layer of orange mousse mixture. Chill at least 2 hours or until firmly set.

Just before serving, carefully remove paper collar from dish. Press the remaining macaroon crumbs around the sides of the soufflé; decorate the top with rosettes of whipped cream and add the tiny macaroons, if you like.

Alternative dessert

Coffee Bavarois

3 egg yolks
2 tablespoons sugar
2 cups milk
2–3 teaspoons dry instant coffee or to taste, dissolved in a little water
1 envelope gelatin
¼ cup water
½ cup heavy cream, whipped until it holds a soft shape
½ cup heavy cream, stiffly whipped (for decoration)
Suchard sauce (for serving)

Plain mold (1 quart capacity); pastry bag and medium star tube

Method
Beat the egg yolks and sugar in a bowl until thick and light. Scald the milk with the instant coffee, stir into the egg yolk mixture and return to the saucepan. Heat gently, stirring constantly, until the custard thickens enough to coat the back of a spoon.
Watchpoint: do not boil or it will curdle.

Strain the custard, sprinkle with a little sugar to prevent a skin from forming on top and let cool.

Sprinkle the gelatin over the water in a small pan and let stand 5 minutes until spongy. Dissolve it over a pan of hot water and stir into the custard. Set the custard over a pan of ice water and stir until cold and on the point of setting. Stir in the lightly whipped cream and pour into the lightly oiled mold. Cover and chill at least 2 hours or until set.

To serve, pull the edges of the Bavarois gently away from the sides of the mold to loosen it and turn out on a platter. Coat the top and sides with whipped cream and mark the top in a wavy pattern with the end of a round-bladed knife. Put the remaining cream in a pastry bag fitted with a medium star tube and decorate the top or the base of the Bavarois with rosettes. Serve with Suchard sauce.

Suchard Sauce

6 squares (6 oz) unsweetened chocolate, chopped
1½ cups water
½ cup sugar
pinch of salt
½ teaspoon vanilla

Method
Melt the chocolate with the water in a pan over low heat, stirring occasionally. When it is smooth, add the sugar and salt and stir until dissolved. Bring the sauce to a boil and simmer, uncovered, until it is rich and syrupy and thick enough to coat the back of a spoon. Take from the heat, stir in the vanilla and let cool.

Noisettes of lamb Henri IV, topped with Béarnaise butter, are served with potato croquettes (recipe is on pages 58–59)

CLASSIC ENTREES (2)

Classic entrées are just as appropriate today for parties as they were when created many years ago. The following entrées are main dishes of steak, veal and lamb garnished with vegetables so that no other accompaniment is needed — they are easy to serve and with their colorful contrasting garnishes they taste as tempting as they look.

When serving classic entrées, it used to be the custom to make one more portion than the number of people at the table to allow for a second helping and to avoid embarrassing the last person to be served. To follow this custom, increase meat or poultry servings and the individual garnishes such as croûtes or artichoke hearts in these recipes; leave quantities of sauces the same.

Tournedos Clamart

4 tournedos steaks, cut 1–1½ inches thick
4 slices of white bread, crusts removed, cut into circles same size as tournedos (for croûtes)
4 tablespoons oil and butter, mixed (for frying)

For garnish
4 cooked artichoke bottoms, fresh, frozen or canned
5 tablespoons butter
1½ cups fresh or frozen shelled peas
½ teaspoon sugar
sprig of mint (optional)
4 mushrooms, trimmed
salt and pepper
½ cup white wine
1½ cups espagnole sauce

Method
To make garnish: prepare fresh artichoke bottoms (see box) or cook frozen ones according to package directions, or drain canned ones. In a pan melt 1 tablespoon butter and gently warm the artichoke bottoms.

Cook fresh peas with sugar and mint in boiling salted water for 10–15 minutes or cook frozen peas according to package directions with the sugar and mint for flavor. Discard mint, drain peas, refresh and drain again; reheat gently with 1 tablespoon butter. Sauté mushrooms in 1 tablespoon butter and keep warm.

Heat half the oil and butter and fry the croûtes on both sides until golden brown; drain on paper towels and reserve. Wipe out pan, add remaining oil and butter and fry tournedos briskly for 2–3 minutes on each side for rare meat; sprinkle with seasoning after turning them. Put a mushroom on each tournedos and set them on the croûtes; arrange on a platter and keep warm.

Add the wine to the pan, stir to dissolve the juices in pan and boil until reduced by half. Add espagnole sauce and simmer 1 minute. Take from heat and whisk in remaining 2 tablespoons butter, a piece at a time. Taste sauce for seasoning and spoon over tournedos.

Arrange artichoke bottoms between the tournedos, fill them with peas and pile Parisienne potatoes in the center.

For tournedos Clamart, fry steaks briskly in oil and butter for 3 minutes on each side

Tournedos steaks (cut from thinner end of a beef fillet) are small but thick — sometimes cut as thick as 2 inches. They should be completely trimmed of fat. One tournedos serves 1 person.

Clamart garnish always refers to artichoke bottoms filled with peas. Clamart is a district near Paris where peas used to be grown.

Tournedos Parisienne

4 tournedos steaks, cut 1–1½ inches thick
4 slices of white bread, crusts removed, cut into circles same size as tournedos (for croûtes)
4 tablespoons oil and butter, mixed (for frying)
1 can (4 oz) firm pâté de foie (liver pâté)
3 tablespoons brandy
salt and pepper
2 cups (½ lb) small mushrooms, trimmed
½ cup heavy cream
2 cups espagnole sauce

Method
In a heavy skillet heat half the oil and butter and fry the croûtes until golden brown on both sides; drain on paper towels and reserve. Beat the pâté with 1 tablespoon brandy until soft and spread on the croûtes; arrange on a serving platter and keep warm.

Wipe out the skillet, heat the remaining oil and butter and fry the tournedos briskly for 2–3 minutes on each side for rare meat; sprinkle with seasoning after turning them. Set tournedos on the croûtes.

Add the mushrooms to the pan and cook briskly for 1 minute. Add the remaining brandy, cream and espagnole sauce, bring to a boil, simmer 1 minute, taste for seasoning and spoon a little of the mushrooms and espagnole sauce over the tournedos to coat them. Serve the remaining sauce and mushrooms separately.

A recipe for Espagnole Sauce is given in Volume 2.

The garnish **Parisienne** usually refers to small white mushrooms called champignons de Paris in French. They are often used for garnish because they look attractive. Wipe them with a damp cloth and trim stems level with caps so mushrooms keep their shape.

For Parisienne potatoes: peel 4 large potatoes, scoop out balls with ball cutter; blanch in boiling, salted water and drain. Cook in 1 tablespoon butter, shaking pan to brown them evenly.

Artichoke Bottoms

To prepare artichoke bottoms: cut the stalks from large artichokes and pull away the lower leaves. Cut the tops off remaining leaves, leaving about 1 inch at the base. Cook artichokes in boiling salted water for 20–25 minutes or until tender, drain and cool slightly.

Pull away the remaining leaves and scoop out the hairy chokes with a teaspoon.

Tournedos Clamart are garnished with mushrooms and artichoke bottoms filled with cooked peas. Parisienne potatoes are piled in the center

Tournedos Chasseur

4 tournedos steaks, cut 1–1½ inches thick
4 slices of white bread, crusts removed, cut into circles same size as tournedos (for croûtes)
4 tablespoons oil and butter, mixed (for frying)
½ cup white wine
1 teaspoon tarragon
1 tablespoon chopped parsley

For sauce
1 cup (¼ lb) mushrooms
2 tablespoons butter
2 shallots, finely chopped
2 teaspoons flour
1½ teaspoons tomato paste
1 cup well-flavored beef stock
salt and pepper

Method
To make the sauce: trim the mushroom stems level with the caps and finely slice the caps. In a small skillet or frying pan heat butter and cook shallot gently until soft; add mushrooms and sauté until lightly brown, stirring so the mixture does not burn. Stir in flour and, after a few seconds, add tomato paste, stock and seasoning. Bring to a boil, stirring, and simmer 10–15 minutes until sauce is glossy and slightly thickened.

In a heavy skillet heat half the oil and butter, fry croûtes on both sides until golden brown, drain on paper towels, and reserve.

Wipe out the pan, heat the remaining oil and butter and fry the tournedos briskly for 2–3 minutes on each side for rare steak; sprinkle with seasoning after turning them. Set each tournedos on a croûte, arrange on a platter and keep warm.

Discard any fat from the pan, add white wine to the pan, stir to dissolve the juices and simmer 1–2 minutes. Add mushroom sauce, simmer 1–2 minutes, add the herbs, taste for seasoning and spoon over the tournedos. Serve very hot with Parisienne potatoes.

Chasseur means 'hunter-style, and refers to a mushroom garnish that is flavored with shallots and white wine.

To coat a dish with sauce means to spoon just enough sauce over and into the dish to cover the food and the bottom of the platter. The base of the dish should not be visible but the food should not be swimming in sauce.

Curried Escalopes

4–8 veal escalopes (about 1½ lb)
3 tablespoons butter
salt and pepper
1 small onion, finely chopped
1 teaspoon curry powder (or to taste)
¼ cup sherry
2 teaspoons flour
½ cup well-flavored stock
1 cup (¼ lb) mushrooms, trimmed
3 tablespoons heavy cream

Method
In a large skillet heat the butter until foaming, add the veal and sauté 3–4 minutes on each side until golden brown; sprinkle with seasoning after turning them. Remove the escalopes and keep warm.

Reduce the heat, add the onion and curry powder to pan and cook gently for 1–2 minutes, stirring. Pour in the sherry and boil until it is reduced by half.

Take the pan from the heat, stir in the flour and pour in the stock. Bring to a boil, stirring, add the mushrooms (whole or sliced, depending on their size) and the veal. Cover the pan and simmer gently for 7–8 minutes. Pour in the cream, bring just to a boil, taste for seasoning and transfer to a serving dish. Serve the veal with paprika rice.

Paprika Rice

1 cup rice
2 teaspoons paprika
1 tablespoon butter

Method
Cook rice in plenty of boiling salted water for 10–12 minutes or until just tender. Drain, rinse with hot water, drain again and spread out to dry in a warm place.

In a frying pan heat the butter, add the paprika and cook gently, stirring, for ½ minute. Add the rice and cook, stirring with a fork, until rice is hot and well coated with paprika butter.

Escalopes Sauté à l'Anglaise

4–8 veal escalopes (about 1½ lb)
¼ cup seasoned flour (made with ¼ teaspoon salt and pinch of pepper)
1 egg, beaten to mix
1 cup fresh white breadcrumbs
¼ cup clarified butter

For garnish
1½ lb fresh asparagus or 2 packages frozen asparagus
4 slices of cooked ham
5 tablespoons butter
juice of ½ small lemon
salt and pepper

Method
Coat the escalopes in seasoned flour, brush them with beaten egg and coat with breadcrumbs, pressing them in well.

For garnish: trim fresh asparagus, cook in simmering salted water for 7–8 minutes or until tender and drain; cook frozen asparagus according to package directions, drain, cut in half and keep hot.

Melt 1 tablespoon butter (not clarified) in a frying pan and gently sauté the ham for 1–2 minutes, then keep warm.

In a large skillet or frying pan heat the clarified butter and sauté the escalopes for 3–4 minutes on each side until golden brown, turning only once. Arrange them, overlapping, on a platter with a slice of ham between each escalope (cut slices of ham in half if the escalopes are small). Arrange the asparagus in the center or at one side of the platter and keep warm.

Wipe out the skillet, heat the remaining unclarified butter and cook to a noisette (nut-brown). At once add the lemon juice with seasoning and pour over the escalopes while still foaming. Serve immediately.

For veal escalopes sauté à l'Anglaise, arrange sautéed veal and ham slices, overlapping, on a platter and keep warm

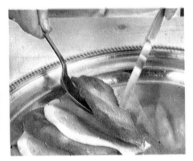

Veal escalopes sauté à l'Anglaise are ready to serve, with a garnish of asparagus

Paupiettes de Veau Bayonne
(Stuffed Veal Rolls Bayonne)

4–8 veal escalopes
(about 1½ lb)
1 tablespoon butter
1 large onion, sliced
1 large carrot, sliced
1½ cups well-flavored stock

For filling
1 cup (½ lb) raw or cooked
Virginia ham, ground or
finely chopped
1½ tablespoons butter
1½ tablespoons flour
½ cup milk
salt and pepper
pinch of ground mace
1 egg, beaten to mix
1 tablespoon heavy cream

For sauce and garnish
4 medium tomatoes
1 clove of garlic, crushed
1 bay leaf
2 teaspoons tomato paste
1 tablespoon chopped parsley

Paupiettes are thin slices of meat spread with stuffing, then rolled and tied to form cylinders. The lightly smoked ham of Bayonne is eaten thinly sliced and raw as an appetizer. Virginia ham is a good substitute here.

Method
Cut large escalopes in half.

To make filling: in a saucepan melt butter, stir in flour off the heat and pour in milk. Bring to a boil, stirring, season, add mace, simmer 2 minutes, cover and let cool. Pound ham in a mortar and pestle and work in the cool sauce. Or instead of pounding, work ham and sauce for a few seconds in a blender. Stir in beaten egg and cream with pepper to taste and spread stuffing on the slices of veal. Roll up neatly and tie paupiettes with string.

In a flameproof casserole heat the butter and cook the onion and carrot, covered, for 5–7 minutes or until soft. Set paupiettes on top, pour over the stock, cover pan and braise in a moderate oven (350°F) for 30 minutes or until the paupiettes are tender.

To make sauce and garnish: wipe 2 tomatoes, slice and squeeze out seeds. Scald and peel remaining tomatoes, discard seeds and cut flesh into strips. Cook sliced tomatoes in a small pan with garlic, bay leaf, seasoning and tomato paste, stirring until mixture is very soft, then work through a strainer.

Take out paupiettes, discard strings, arrange them in a serving dish and keep warm. Simmer the cooking liquid until reduced by half, strain and stir into strained tomato mixture. Bring to a boil, simmer until slightly thickened, add tomato strips and parsley, heat thoroughly and taste for seasoning. Spoon over and around the paupiettes.

Anna Judic was a celebrated French actress in the 19th century. She had several dishes named for her, said to have been created by the great Chef Escoffier. One of the best known is this garnish for entrées.

Veal Chops Judic

4 rib or loin veal chops
1 medium onion, quartered
1 carrot, sliced
2 cups chicken stock
1 bay leaf
salt and pepper
1 tablespoon butter
1 tablespoon flour
1 egg yolk, mixed with
3 tablespoons heavy cream
(for liaison)

For garnish
large head of Boston lettuce
3 tablespoons butter
12 scallions, trimmed and cut
in 1 inch lengths
2–3 tablespoons chicken stock
10–12 small new potatoes,
peeled
2 teaspoons chopped parsley
1 teaspoon chopped mint
(optional)

Method
Trim any fat from the chops and set them in a shallow pan with the onion and carrot. Pour over the stock, add the bay leaf and seasoning, cover the pan and simmer 20–30 minutes or until the chops are tender.

To make garnish: wash and trim lettuce, place in a colander and pour over a kettle of boiling water. Refresh, drain well, cut lettuce in 4–5 wedges and press dry with paper towels. In a flameproof casserole, melt 2 tablespoons butter, add scallions, cover and cook slowly for 5 minutes or until tender. Arrange lettuce on top, season and spoon over stock. Press a piece of buttered foil on top of lettuce, add lid and bake in a moderate oven (350°F) for 30–40 minutes or until lettuce is very tender.

Cook the potatoes in boiling salted water for 10–15 minutes or until just tender; drain.

When the chops are cooked, strain liquid from pan and reserve. Keep the chops warm.

In a saucepan melt 1 tablespoon butter, stir in flour and cook gently until straw-colored. Stir in 1¼ cups reserved cooking liquid, bring to a boil and simmer 5 minutes. Stir a little sauce into the liaison, then return mixture to remaining sauce in pan and heat gently, stirring, until it thickens slightly.

Watchpoint: do not boil.

Take chops from pan, add them to sauce, cover and leave in a warm place for 10 minutes for flavors to blend. Reheat potatoes with remaining tablespoon butter, parsley and mint, if used, and keep warm.

Arrange the chops in a deep serving dish and spoon over the sauce. Lift lettuce and scallions from casserole with a slotted spoon and arrange around chops with new potatoes.

Noisettes of Lamb Henri IV

3–3½ lb rack of lamb
salt and pepper
¼ teaspoon thyme
¼ teaspoon marjoram
2 teaspoons chopped parsley
6–8 slices of white bread,
crusts removed, cut into
circles same size as noisettes
(for croûtes)
2–4 tablespoons oil and butter,
mixed (for frying)
¼ cup sherry (optional)
¼ cup stock (optional)

To finish
1½ lb fresh spinach or
2 packages frozen spinach
potato croquettes
1 tablespoon butter
pinch of nutmeg
¾ cup Béarnaise sauce

Method

To make noisettes: remove the chop bones, using a small sharp knife and working in short sharp strokes. Keep knife close to the bone to avoid cutting into the meat. Season the cut surface of meat, sprinkle with the herbs and roll up, starting at the lean side. Trim off fat if there is more than enough to wrap once around the lean meat. Tie the roll securely at 1–1½ inch intervals with fine string; cut between each tied section to make a 'noisette' or nut.

Fry croûtes in half the oil and butter until brown on both sides; drain on paper towels and reserve.

Wash fresh spinach thoroughly, remove the stems and cook in boiling salted water for 5–6 minutes or cook frozen spinach according to package directions. Drain well and press between 2 plates to remove all the water. Make potato croquettes and keep warm. Make Béarnaise sauce and keep warm in a water bath.

Broil the noisettes for 4–5 minutes on each side for medium cooked meat or fry them in remaining oil and butter for 2–3 minutes on each side; remove the strings. Sprinkle them with seasoning, set on croûtes and arrange down one side of a large platter.

If frying noisettes, discard any fat remaining in pan and dissolve pan juices with sherry and stock. Simmer 4–5 minutes, taste for seasoning and serve in a separate sauce boat.

Toss the spinach with 1 tablespoon butter until it is very hot, season and add nutmeg; pile in the center of platter. Arrange potato croquettes on other side, spoon a little Béarnaise sauce over each noisette and serve at once.

Béarnaise Sauce

3 tablespoons wine vinegar
6 peppercorns
½ bay leaf
1 blade of mace
1 slice of onion
2 egg yolks
½ cup butter
salt and pepper
1 teaspoon meat glaze
1 teaspoon tarragon
1 teaspoon chervil
1 teaspoon chopped parsley
pinch of chopped chives, or
    little grated onion

Makes ¾ cup.

Method

Put vinegar, peppercorns, bay leaf, mace and slice of onion into a pan; boil until reduced to 1 tablespoon. Set aside.

Place yolks in a small bowl with ½ tablespoon butter and a pinch of salt and beat until thick. Strain in vinegar, set bowl on a pan of boiling water, turn off heat and stir until beginning to thicken.

Add remaining softened butter in small pieces, beating well after each addition. Add meat glaze, herbs and chives or onion and season with pepper. Finished sauce should be the consistency of whipped cream.

Potato Croquettes

Cook 3 medium potatoes in boiling salted water for 15 minutes or until tender. Drain; work through a strainer or ricer. Return to pan, beat in 1 tablespoon butter, 1 egg yolk, 2 tablespoons hot milk, salt and pepper. Cool mixture, roll on a floured board into a 1 inch thick cylinder. Cut into 2 inch lengths.

Roll croquettes in flour, seasoned with salt and pepper, brush with 1 egg, beaten to mix with ½ teaspoon salt. Coat with dry white breadcrumbs; fry in butter, turning so they brown evenly, or fry in deep fat (375°F on a fat thermometer). Drain well on paper towels.

Noisettes of Lamb Milanaise

2½–3 lb rack of lamb, boned
salt and pepper
1 tablespoon chopped mixed
    herbs (thyme, rosemary and
    parsley)
¼ cup clarified butter or oil
    (for frying)
½–¾ cup white wine or stock
    (to finish)–optional

For spaghetti Milanaise
½ lb spaghetti
2 tablespoons butter
½ cup (¼ lb) cooked ham, cut in
    julienne strips
1 cup (¼ lb) mushrooms, sliced
    and sautéed in 1 tablespoon
    butter

For tomato sauce
3 tomatoes, quartered and
    seeded or 2 cups (1 lb)
    canned tomatoes, crushed
3 tablespoons butter
1 onion, sliced
1 carrot, sliced
2 tablespoons flour
1½ cups stock
1–2 cloves of garlic, crushed
2 teaspoons tomato paste
bouquet garni

Method

Season cut surface of lamb and sprinkle with herbs. Roll up, tie and cut into noisettes.

To make tomato sauce: melt butter in a pan, add onion and carrot and cook slowly until soft but not brown. Stir in flour, pour in stock and add tomatoes, garlic, tomato paste, bouquet garni and seasoning. Bring to a boil and simmer 20–30 minutes; strain and return to pan. Boil sauce, stirring occasionally, until thick and concentrated in flavor. Keep warm.

To make spaghetti Milanaise: cook spaghetti in plenty of boiling salted water for 8–10 minutes or until only just tender 'al dente'. Drain, rinse with hot water, drain thoroughly and reheat with the butter. Add tomato sauce with ham and cooked mushrooms, taste for seasoning and keep warm.

In a skillet heat clarified butter or oil and fry noisettes over medium heat for 5–6 minutes on each side until a light golden brown. Season noisettes when turning to brown the other side.

Watchpoint: if noisettes are browned but not sufficiently cooked to your taste (the juice that runs out when you prick them with a fork should be pink for medium done or clear for well done), set them on a rack over skillet and bake in a hot oven (425°F) for 4–5 minutes to complete cooking.

Arrange noisettes around a warm platter and pile spaghetti Milanaise in the center. If you like, make a gravy by pouring off the fat from the pan and dissolving the skillet juices in a little white wine or stock, then pour over the noisettes. Serve with a green salad, if you like.

Melon salad makes a very decorative lunch dish. It can also be served with cream cheese dressing. (Recipe is on page 67)

SALADS FOR LIGHT LUNCHES

Light and easy to prepare ahead, salads have double appeal for lunch. Some salad combinations are traditional but you can invent and improvise many others with ingredients that happen to be available.

Breton salad is garnished with quarters of hard-cooked eggs and chopped mixed herbs

Breton Salad

3 medium carrots, diced
3 medium white turnips, diced
$\frac{1}{3}$ lb green beans, cut in
  diamonds
3 medium potatoes, diced
$\frac{1}{4}$ cup vinaigrette dressing

For mock mayonnaise
$\frac{1}{2}$ teaspoon dry mustard
$\frac{1}{2}$ teaspoon sugar
salt and pepper
$\frac{1}{3}$ cup unsweetened evaporated
  milk
$\frac{1}{3}$ cup oil
2 tablespoons vinegar

For garnish
1 hard-cooked egg, quartered
1 tablespoon mixed chopped
  herbs (parsley, chives,
  marjoram)

Method
To make mock mayonnaise: in a small bowl put the mustard and sugar with seasoning and stir in the evaporated milk until smooth. Gradually whisk in the oil, then whisk in the vinegar so the dressing emulsifies and thickens slightly; taste for seasoning.

Cook the carrots, turnips, beans and potatoes in boiling salted water for 6–8 minutes or until just tender; drain, refresh and drain again. Mix with vinaigrette dressing and let stand 10 minutes.

Add the mock mayonnaise, toss carefully so the vegetables are coated and taste for seasoning. Pile the mixture in a bowl, garnish with quarters of hard-cooked egg and sprinkle with herbs.

Tomato Chartreuse with Shrimps

For tomato chartreuse
4 cups tomato juice or 1 can
  (2 lb) tomatoes, crushed
strip of lemon rind
1 teaspoon tomato paste
1 clove of garlic, bruised
1 bay leaf
6 peppercorns
salt and pepper
sugar
2 envelopes gelatin
$\frac{1}{2}$ cup white wine or cold water
juice of 1 lemon (or to taste)

For dressing
6 tablespoons olive oil
2 tablespoons wine vinegar
$\frac{1}{2}$ cup finely ground walnuts
pinch of dry mustard

For garnish
1 lb cooked peeled shrimps
bunch of watercress

Ring mold (1 quart capacity)

Method
In a saucepan combine the tomato juice or tomatoes with the lemon rind, tomato paste, garlic, bay leaf, peppercorns and salt and sugar to taste. Bring slowly to a boil, simmer 5 minutes and work through a strainer.

Sprinkle the gelatin over the wine or water and let stand 5 minutes until spongy. Add to the hot tomato mixture and stir until dissolved. Add the lemon juice, taste for seasoning and pour into the wet ring mold. Cover and chill at least 2 hours or until firmly set.

To make the dressing: whisk together oil and vinegar, stir in ground walnuts, a pinch of dry mustard and season to taste. Toss with the shrimps and pile in a serving dish.

Just before serving, unmold the tomato chartreuse, arrange the watercress in the center and serve the shrimp mixture separately.

Salad Alice

bunch of celery, cut in
  julienne strips
$\frac{1}{4}$ cup whole blanched almonds
1 head of escarole
3 Delicious or other dessert
  apples

For dressing
2 oz Gorgonzola or Roquefort
  cheese
$\frac{3}{4}$ cup heavy cream
juice of $\frac{1}{2}$ lemon (or to taste)
$\frac{1}{2}$ teaspoon sugar (or to taste)
salt and pepper

Method
Soak the celery in ice water for 30 minutes to make it crisp, then drain well. Pour boiling water over the almonds, let stand 5 minutes, drain and split them lengthwise. Break the escarole into pieces, wash and dry well.

To make the dressing: work cheese until soft; gradually beat in the cream. Add lemon juice and sugar and season to taste.

To serve: put the celery, escarole and almonds in a bowl. Wipe the apples, core and slice them into the bowl without paring. Pour over the dressing, toss the salad until well coated with dressing, pile in a salad bowl and serve.

Swiss Salad

$1\frac{1}{2}$ lb fresh spinach, washed
  and stems removed
$\frac{1}{2}$ lb sliced Gruyère cheese, cut
  in squares
1 tablespoon oil
1 tablespoon vinegar
salt and pepper
1 tablespoon chopped chives

For dressing
juice of 1 lemon
pinch of sugar
$\frac{1}{4}$ cup oil
$\frac{3}{4}$ cup heavy cream

Serve with hot garlic loaf.

Method
Cook spinach in plenty of boiling salted water for 4–5 minutes, drain and press thoroughly between 2 plates to remove water. Mix with oil and vinegar, season and spread in a serving dish or salad bowl. Arrange cheese on top.

To make the dressing: whisk the lemon juice with a pinch of salt, pepper and sugar, beat in the oil; gradually beat in the cream so the dressing thickens slightly. Taste for seasoning and spoon over the cheese. Sprinkle with chopped chives.

Vinaigrette Dressing

For $\frac{1}{2}$ cup: mix 2 tablespoons vinegar (any of the following types: red or white wine, cider or tarragon) with $\frac{1}{2}$ teaspoon salt and $\frac{1}{2}$ teaspoon freshly ground black pepper. Gradually add 6 tablespoons oil, preferably olive or peanut, whisking until dressing thickens slightly. Taste for seasoning.

Roman Salad with Noodles

1 lb cooked ham, cut in finger-sized strips
½ lb fettucine verde (green noodles)
2 cups (½ lb) very fresh mushrooms, quartered or thickly sliced
½ cup ripe olives, pitted

For dressing
2 tablespoons red wine vinegar
salt and pepper
6 tablespoons olive oil
¼ cup chili sauce, or ketchup
1 tablespoon chopped parsley
1 teaspoon mixed herbs (oregano, thyme)

For garnish
3 medium tomatoes, peeled and sliced
1 cup mayonnaise
½ teaspoon Dijon-style mustard (or to taste)

Method
Cook the noodles in plenty of boiling salted water for 8—10 minutes or until just tender 'al dente'. Drain, rinse with cold water until shiny and drain again.

To make the dressing: mix the vinegar with the seasoning, then whisk in the oil, chili sauce or ketchup and herbs.

Put the ham in a bowl with the noodles, mushrooms and olives, pour over the dressing and mix carefully. Pile the salad in a serving dish and arrange the tomato slices around the edge.

Thin the mayonnaise with a little boiling water until it pours fairly easily; beat in mustard to taste and serve separately with the salad.

Mushroom and Gruyère Salad

3 cups (¾ lb) mushrooms
½ lb Gruyère cheese, cut in julienne strips
2 tablespoons olive oil
½ cup vinaigrette dressing (made with olive oil and lemon juice) – see page 63
2 shallots or scallions, finely chopped
1½ cups shelled baby lima beans or 1 package frozen lima beans
salt and pepper
lettuce leaves or bunch of watercress

Method
Trim the mushroom stems level with the caps. In a skillet heat olive oil and sauté mushroom caps gently until just tender. Drain them and while still hot toss with vinaigrette dressing and add the shallots or scallions. Let cool.

Cook beans in boiling salted water for 15—18 minutes or until tender or cook frozen beans according to package directions. Drain, refresh beans with cold water and drain again thoroughly.

Add the beans and cheese to the mushroom mixture, mix well and add more seasoning, if necessary. Arrange lettuce leaves or sprigs of watercress around a salad bowl, pile the salad in the center and serve.

Harlequin Salad

3 medium potatoes, peeled and diced
3 medium carrots, peeled and diced
¼ lb green beans, cut in 1-inch lengths
1 cup fresh or frozen green peas
½ lb cooked ham, diced
1 cup mayonnaise
salt and pepper

For garnish
3 hard-cooked eggs
1 cup (¼ lb) mushrooms
½ tablespoon butter
squeeze of lemon juice
¼ cup water
¼ cup pitted green olives, finely chopped
1 medium tomato

Method
Cook the potatoes and carrots in boiling salted water for 8—10 minutes or until just tender and drain. Cook the green beans with fresh peas in boiling salted water for 6—8 minutes or until just tender, drain, refresh and drain thoroughly. Cook frozen peas according to package directions and drain. Let cool.

Combine all the vegetables with the ham, add the mayonnaise and mix well. Taste for seasoning and pile in a salad bowl, smoothing the top.

To prepare the garnish: separate the egg whites from the yolks; finely chop the whites and work the yolks through a sieve. Put the mushrooms in a pan with the butter, lemon juice and water, cover and cook over high heat for 2—3 minutes or until tender. Drain and chop the mushrooms finely.

Spread the chopped egg whites, egg yolks, olives and mushrooms over the salad completely to reflect pie-shaped wedges. Using the blade of a knife, make a clean insertion between each wedge. Cut the tomato in half, scoop out the center and cut the edges in points to make a flower; set it in the center of the salad.

Veal and Pepper Salad

3—4 veal escalopes (about ¾ lb)
3 green peppers, cored, seeded, cut in strips and blanched
1½ tablespoons olive oil
2 shallots, finely chopped
1½ teaspoons tomato paste
6 tablespoons sherry
2 cups (½ lb) mushrooms
1 cup (½ lb) cooked ham, cut in julienne strips
5—6 tablespoons vinaigrette dressing (see page 63)
salt and pepper
3 medium tomatoes, peeled and sliced

Method
In a skillet heat the oil and sauté the escalopes for 2—3 minutes on each side or until golden brown. Add shallot, stir in tomato paste and sherry, cover pan and simmer 5 minutes. Add mushrooms and cook 3 minutes longer.

Let the mixture cool, then cut the escalopes into julienne strips. Mix all ingredients together, except the tomatoes, season to taste and pile in a serving dish. Garnish with tomato slices.

Harlequin salad is an attractive lunch dish

Crab and rice salad is sprinkled with coarsely chopped walnuts to serve

Crab and Rice Salad

1 cup ($\frac{1}{2}$ lb) crab meat
1 cup rice
1 clove of garlic, cut in half
1 red or green pepper, cored, seeded, cut in fine strips and blanched
$\frac{1}{2}$ cup pitted ripe olives, halved
1 cup ($\frac{1}{4}$ lb) very fresh mushrooms, sliced
salt and pepper
$\frac{1}{4}$ cup coarsely chopped walnuts

For dressing
juice of 1 lemon
4–5 tablespoons olive oil
black pepper, freshly ground

Method
Cook rice in boiling salted water for 10–12 minutes or until just tender, drain, rinse with hot water, drain thoroughly and spread out to dry in a warm place.

To make the dressing: whisk the lemon juice, oil and pepper together with a little salt; mix with rice while still warm.

Rub a cut clove of garlic

For crab and rice salad, cut the red bell pepper in julienne strips and add to the rice with the flaked crab meat

around a salad bowl, then discard. When the rice is cold, transfer it to a salad bowl. Flake the crab meat with a fork, stir it into the rice with strips of pepper, olives and raw mushrooms. Taste the salad for seasoning, pile in the center of the bowl and sprinkle over the walnuts.

Salad Japonaise

1 head of Boston lettuce
2 oranges
3 medium tomatoes, peeled, seeded and cut in quarters
1 small pineapple, peeled, cored and cut in chunks, or 1 can (8$\frac{1}{2}$ oz) pineapple chunks, drained
1$\frac{1}{2}$ cups tarragon cream dressing
1 tablespoon chopped parsley (optional)

Serve salad Japonaise with sliced cold roast chicken, turkey or ham or cut the meat in julienne strips and mix with the salad.

Method
Wash and dry the lettuce and arrange the leaves on individual plates, breaking the spines so the leaves lie flat. Cut the rind, making sure you remove all the pith, from the oranges with a serrated-edge knife and divide oranges into sections.

Arrange the orange sections, tomato quarters and pineapple chunks on one side of the plates and arrange chicken, turkey or ham on the other side. Spoon over the dressing and sprinkle with parsley, if you like.

Tarragon Cream Dressing

For 2 cups: in a bowl or the top of a double boiler beat 1 large egg with a fork until mixed. Add 2 tablespoons sugar and gradually stir in 3 tablespoons tarragon vinegar. Stand the bowl over a pan of boiling water or heat the water in the bottom of double boiler and cook the mixture, stirring constantly, until it begins to thicken. Take pan or double boiler off the heat and continue stirring. When the mixture is thick, lift the container from the hot water and stir 1 minute longer. Season lightly and cool. Whip $\frac{3}{4}$ cup heavy cream until it holds a soft shape and fold into the cool vinegar mixture. Taste for seasoning.

This dressing can be made, without adding the cream, in large quantities and stored in an airtight container in the refrigerator for up to 3 weeks. Add the whipped cream just before serving.

Melon Salad with Cream Cheese Dressing

1 large Crenshaw or Persian melon
1 cantaloupe melon
4 navel oranges

For cream cheese dressing
1 package (3 oz) cream cheese
$\frac{1}{2}$ cup sour cream
2 tablespoons mayonnaise

For sprinkling
$\frac{1}{4}$ cup light brown sugar
1 teaspoons ground cinnamon
1 teaspoon ground allspice

Method
Cut the Crenshaw or Persian melon in quarters or cut out 2 wedges, leaving a handle in the center to form a basket. Scoop out the flesh of the melon with a ball cutter, discarding the seeds, and scrape the shell clean. Decorate the edges of the melon basket or quarters by cutting into points with a knife. Cut the cantaloupe melon in half, discard the seeds and scoop out the flesh with a ball cutter. Divide the oranges into sections. Combine the fruit and chill it thoroughly. Also chill the melon basket or quarters.

To make the dressing: work the cream cheese through a strainer and beat in the sour cream and mayonnaise, or beat the cheese with the cream and mayonnaise in an electric blender. Mix the brown sugar and spices for sprinkling and pile in a serving bowl.

A short time before serving, pile the fruit in the melon basket or quarters. Serve the dressing and spiced sugar separately.

Trout meunière is a simple dish of trout served in a rich noisette butter (recipe is on page 70)

TROUT MEUNIERE IS A CLASSIC TREAT

Trout Meunière

Braised Veal Orloff
Boiled Rice
Fresh Lima Beans or Brussels Sprouts

Almond & Apricot Flan

~

White wine for trout – Erbacher (Germany)
or Johannisberg Riesling (California)

White wine for veal – Meursault (Côte de Beaune)
or Pinot Chardonnay (California)

Start your menu with the classic trout meunière – topped with fresh herbs in noisette butter – or a special carrot soup flavored with orange juice. As an entrée spread carved braised veal with soubise purée and spoon over mornay sauce to make a party surprise. Dessert is an almond pastry flan filled with apricots and almonds.

Fresh trout deserve a splendid white wine and those from vineyards at Erbach in Germany's Rheingau district are among the very best. For an American alternative, try a Johannisberg Riesling from a good Napa Valley vineyard. A fine choice of white wine to complement the veal is a Meursault from France's Côte de Beaune or a Pinot Chardonnay from California's Livermore Valley.

TIMETABLE

Day before
Make stock for veal; braise veal and store in pot in refrigerator.
Make chicken stock for soup.
Make almond pastry dough and store in plastic bag in refrigerator.
Poach apricots, if using fresh ones, and leave in juice.

Morning
Make soubise purée and prepare mornay sauce for veal.
Carve veal, spread soubise purée on slices and reshape the meat; coat with mornay sauce and make gravy.
Roll out dough and bake almond pastry. Drain apricots and prepare apricot glaze, split blanched almonds; do not assemble flan.
Wash, clean and trim trout and refrigerate; chop parsley and fresh herbs and wrap tightly. Squeeze lemon juice.
Make soup and refrigerate.
Boil rice if serving, drain, dry and leave in buttered dish, covered with buttered foil, ready for reheating.
Shell lima beans or prepare Brussels sprouts, if serving. Wrap tightly and refrigerate.
Assemble ingredients for final cooking from 7 p.m. for dinner around 8 p.m.

Order of Work
7:00
Set oven at moderate (350°F). Whip and flavor cream, assemble almond and apricot flan, brush with glaze and refrigerate.
7:15
Put veal in oven to brown.
7:30
Cook lima beans or Brussels sprouts.
Put rice in oven to reheat.
Cook mushrooms for veal garnish and keep warm.
7:45
Drain and refresh beans or sprouts.
Sauté trout and pour over meunière butter.
Heat soup or pour cold soup into soup bowls.
Turn oven to low; garnish veal with mushrooms and keep warm.
Reheat gravy.
8:00
Serve first course.
Reheat lima beans or Brussels sprouts in butter just before serving.

> You will find that **cooking times** given in the individual recipes for these dishes have sometimes been adapted in the timetable to help you when cooking and serving this menu as a party meal.

Trout Meunière

4 rainbow trout, with heads left on
$\frac{1}{4}$ cup seasoned flour (made with $\frac{1}{4}$ teaspoon salt and pinch of pepper)
3 tablespoons butter

To finish
2 tablespoons butter
juice of $\frac{1}{2}$ lemon
salt and pepper
1 tablespoon chopped parsley
1 teaspoon chopped fresh herbs (chives, thyme, chervil) – optional

For this dish use only fresh herbs (when in season) as dried herbs will spoil the flavor.

Method
Wash the trout and clean them thoroughly; pat dry with paper towels. Cut off fins and trim or 'vandyke' the tails in a neat 'V'. If the fish are large, score them once or twice on either side and then roll them in the seasoned flour.

Heat a heavy frying pan or skillet, add the 3 tablespoons butter and, when it starts to foam, put in the fish and cook over medium heat until golden brown on both sides, turning once. Allow about 6 minutes cooking on each side.
Watchpoint: use a heavy frying pan or skillet so it can be heated before the butter is put in the pan; then there will be enough heat to start cooking the fish before the butter browns.

Place the cooked trout, without draining, on a hot platter. Traditionally, the fish should be served on a long oval platter.

To make meunière butter:

wipe out the skillet or frying pan with paper towels, add the butter and cook slowly to a nut-brown (noisette). At once add the lemon juice, seasoning, parsley and herbs, if used, and pour meunière butter, foaming, over the trout. Serve at once.

Wash, clean and pat dry trout, then cut off fins with scissors. Trim or 'vandyke' the tails in a neat 'V'

Coat trout in seasoned flour and cook them in a pan of foaming butter until they are golden brown

Potage crème d'or, flavored with the juice of an orange, is garnished with chopped chives

Alternative appetizer

Potage Crème d'Or

5–6 medium young carrots, peeled and sliced
salt and pepper
½ teaspoon sugar
3 tablespoons butter
1 medium onion, finely chopped
5 cups chicken stock
juice of 1 orange
1 cup heavy cream
1 tablespoon chopped chives (for garnish)

Method

Simmer the carrots, covered, in a pan with salt and pepper, sugar and water to cover for 15 minutes or until carrots are tender; drain. If the carrots are old, discard the hard yellow core before cooking.

In a pan melt the butter, add the onion and cook over a low heat until soft but not browned. Add the carrots and cook gently until the butter is absorbed.

Work the carrot mixture through a sieve or food mill or purée in a blender with a little of the stock.

Mix the carrot purée with the remaining stock, orange juice, seasoning and cream and stir gently until well mixed. Taste for seasoning. Chill thoroughly before serving and add the chives.

This soup can also be heated to serve hot.

Watchpoint: if serving the soup hot, do not let it boil after the orange juice and cream have been added or the orange flavor is lessened and the soup may curdle. Sprinkle with chives just before serving.

Braised veal Orloff – the cooked veal is sliced, spread with onion purée and reshaped. Mornay sauce is spooned over the top, the dish is browned in the oven and garnished with mushrooms. Serve with boiled rice and Brussels sprouts

Entrée

Braised Veal Orloff

2½–3 lb boneless veal roast
2 tablespoons butter
1 large onion, diced
2 carrots, diced
1 stalk of celery, diced
salt and pepper
½ cup white wine
1½ cups stock
bouquet garni
1½ teaspoons arrowroot
    (mixed to a paste with
    1 tablespoon cold water)

For soubise purée
2 large onions, chopped
1 tablespoon butter
¼ cup rice
¾ cup stock
1 egg yolk
1 tablespoon heavy cream

For mornay sauce
2 tablespoons butter
1½ tablespoons flour
1 cup milk
2–3 tablespoons grated
    Parmesan cheese
1 tablespoon heavy cream

For garnish
2 cups (½ lb) mushrooms,
    stems trimmed level with
    caps
1 tablespoon butter
squeeze of lemon juice

Method

Set the oven at moderate (350°F).

If not already done, tie the veal neatly with string to keep it in shape during cooking. Melt the butter in a large flameproof casserole, add the diced vegetables, place the veal on top of them and season. Cover the pot and braise in heated oven for 30 minutes.

Pour the wine over the veal, cover and cook for about 30 minutes longer to reduce the wine. Pour in the stock (it should come halfway up the meat) and add the bouquet garni; cover pot with foil, then the lid.

Lower oven heat to moderately low (325°F) and braise the veal for 1½–2 hours or until very tender.

To prepare soubise purée: cook chopped onion in the butter over low heat until soft but not brown. Add the rice, stock and seasoning. Bring to a boil, cover and bake in the oven for about 30 minutes or until rice is very soft.

Watchpoint: the rice is deliberately over-cooked in this recipe.

Work the rice and onion mixture through a sieve or purée in a blender, then stir in the egg yolk and cream.

Make the mornay sauce, season, cover and keep warm.

To prepare garnish: cook mushrooms in 1 tablespoon butter with seasoning and a squeeze of lemon juice for 1–2 minutes, shaking the pan so the mushrooms cook evenly; keep warm.

Take the veal from the casserole and keep warm. Strain the cooking liquid into a small pan, bring to a boil and whisk in the arrowroot paste to thicken it slightly. Taste for seasoning and keep warm.

Carve the veal into three-eighth inch slices, spread each one with soubise purée and reshape the veal in an ovenproof serving dish. Spoon mornay sauce over the top of the meat and bake it in a hot oven (400°F) for 12–15 minutes or until browned. Pour a little of the gravy around the meat and garnish with mushrooms. Serve the remaining gravy separately. Serve with boiled rice, fresh lima beans or Brussels sprouts.

Note: to prepare this dish ahead of time, carve, stuff, reshape the meat, coat it with mornay sauce up to 12 hours in advance and store it in the refrigerator. Cook for 30–40 minutes in a moderate oven (350°F) for the meat to heat and brown.

Accompaniment to entrée

Boiled Rice

Allow ¼ cup rice per person.

In a large pan bring plenty of salted water to a boil — at least 3 quarts per cup of rice — and add a slice of lemon to bleach the rice and add flavor.

Add the rice and boil as fast as possible for 10–12 minutes or until the grains are just tender. Rice overcooks easily, so watch the cooking time carefully. Stir occasionally with a fork during cooking to prevent it from sticking.

To stop the rice cooking, tip it quickly into a colander and drain, or pour ½ cup cold water into the pan and then drain. Rinse thoroughly with hot water to wash away any remaining starch, making several draining holes in the rice with the handle of a wooden spoon. Turn it onto a large platter; leave in a warm place or in a very low oven to dry for at least 15 minutes before serving. Turn rice from time to time with a fork.

For easy reheating, spoon rice into a well-buttered, shallow ovenproof dish which should be small enough for the rice to fill it amply. Place a sheet of buttered paper or foil on top. Reheat the rice, allowing 20 minutes in a moderate oven (350°F) and serve in the same dish.

Dessert

Almond and Apricot Flan

1 lb fresh apricots or 1 can
  (16 oz) halved apricots
sugar syrup for fresh apricots
  (made with 1 cup water and
  3 tablespoons sugar)
2 tablespoons apricot jam
1½ teaspoons arrowroot (mixed
  to a paste with 1 tablespoon
  water) – optional
1 cup heavy cream, stiffly
  whipped and flavored with
  1–2 tablespoons sugar or
  1 tablespoon kirsch
10–12 whole blanched
  almonds, split lengthwise

For almond pastry
½ cup whole blanched almonds,
  ground
1½ cups flour
pinch of salt
2 tablespoons shortening
6 tablespoons butter
3 tablespoons sugar
1 egg yolk
2–3 tablespoons ice water

8–9 inch flan ring

Method

For fresh apricots: make sugar
syrup and bring just to a boil.
Cut apricots in half and
remove the pits. Poach them
in the syrup for 8–12 minutes
or until just tender. Drain
them, reserving the juice and
remove the skins. If using canned apricots, drain them and
reserve the juice.

To prepare almond pastry:
sift flour with the salt, rub
shortening and butter into the
flour with the fingertips until
the mixture resembles fine
crumbs. Stir in the ground
almonds and sugar. Mix the
egg yolk with the water and
stir into the almond mixture.

Work pastry dough lightly
until it is smooth and chill for
30 minutes.

Set the oven at moderately
hot (375°F).

Roll out dough on a lightly
floured board, line the flan ring
with it and bake blind in
heated oven for 15–20 minutes or until the pastry is
firm – do not let it brown.

Work the apricot jam
through a sieve, boil the
juice from the apricots until it
is thick and syrupy and stir in
the apricot jam until melted.
Strain and, if the glaze is too
thin, bring it back to a boil;
stir in the arrowroot paste and
heat until the glaze thickens.
Let cool before using.

When the flan shell is cold,
fill it with the flavored whipped cream and arrange the
apricots and almonds in a
circle on top. Brush the top
generously with the glaze and
let it set before serving.

Fill the cold baked flan shell with flavored whipped cream and put the drained apricot halves and split blanched almonds in circles on top

When the flan is filled with circles of apricots and almonds, brush the top generously with glaze made with thickened apricot juice and jam

Almond and apricot flan is a decorative dessert

Battenburg cake, a traditional British favorite, is an attractive variation of the usual pound cake mixture

CAKES FOR SPECIAL OCCASIONS

Few cooking creations add more to special occasions than a really grand gâteau, decked with frosting, flowers and perhaps a few little meringue mushrooms or a trail of almond paste ivy.

Don't be daunted by the length of the recipes in this feature because the cakes are no more complicated than the parts that combine to make them. However, you do need time and patience because as many as five different basic recipes may be combined to build such spectacular centerpieces as the tub of mushrooms. These cakes keep well so you can make them a day or two ahead.

Battenburg Cake

¼ cup apricot jam glaze
1½ cup quantity of almond
  paste

For pound cake
¾ cup butter
¾ cup sugar
3 eggs
1½ cups cake flour
pinch of salt
1 teaspoon baking powder
1 teaspoon vanilla
1–2 tablespoons milk
few drops of red food coloring

*2 large loaf pans
  (9 X 5 X 3 inches each)*

This cake keeps well in an air-tight container for 5–7 days.

Method
Set oven at moderate (350°F) and grease loaf pans. Line the bottoms with wax paper, grease again and sprinkle the pans with flour, discarding the excess.

Make the cake batter (see Volume 1), divide it in half and color one half pale pink with food coloring. Spread pink batter in one pan and plain in the other. Bake in heated oven for 15–20 minutes or until the cakes test done. Turn out onto a wire rack to cool. When cold, trim each cake and cut it into 2 strips lengthwise. Warm the apricot jam glaze, brush the strips of cake with it and put one pink strip on top of a plain one and vice versa to make a checkered rectangle.

Roll out the almond paste on a lightly sugared board with a rolling pin, shaping it into a neat rectangle the length of the reshaped cake and wide enough to wrap around sides, leaving the ends exposed. Brush top of cake with apricot jam glaze and place it, upside down, on the almond paste. Brush the sides

and base of the cake with glaze and press the almond paste around, arranging the seam neatly along one side.

Turn the cake right side up, scallop the edges of the almond paste with your fingers and lightly score the top in a lattice pattern with the back of a knife.

Almond Paste

1½ cups whole blanched
  almonds, ground
1 cup granulated sugar
1 cup confectioners' sugar
1 egg
2 egg yolks
juice of 1 lemon
1 teaspoon almond extract
1 teaspoon vanilla

Makes 1½ cup quantity of almond paste.

Method
Sift the ground almonds and both sugars into a bowl. Add remaining ingredients and work together kneading well so that the oil is drawn out of the almonds and the paste becomes very smooth. Cover and use as required.

Join together the four strips of pound cake to give the checkered effect characteristic of a Battenburg cake

Set the cake on a sheet of almond paste and brush the sides and base with glaze

Scallop the edges of almond paste and decorate in a lattice pattern by scoring top lightly with the back of a knife

Apricot Jam Glaze

In a saucepan bring slowly to a boil 12 oz of apricot jam with the juice of ½ lemon and 2 tablespoons water. Stir until smooth, simmer 5 minutes, strain and return to the pan. Boil 5 minutes and pour into a jar for storage. If for immediate use, continue boiling until thick, then brush over the cake. If using a smooth jam or jelly with no pieces of fruit, do not add water.

This glaze keeps well, so make 2 cups or more at a time to use as needed.

Quantity Terms
Terms like '1 cup quantity' refer to the amount obtained by using 1 cup of the main ingredient (at the top of the list of ingredients) not 1 cup prepared mixture.

Baby's Ball

3-egg pound cake (see recipe
  for Battenburg cake)
1½ cup quantity of almond
  paste
½ cup apricot jam glaze
blue and red food coloring

Two 7 inch ovenproof bowls

This cake keeps well in an air-tight container for 5–7 days.

Method
Set oven at moderate (350°F) and grease and flour the bowls, discarding the excess.

Make the cake batter, divide it in half and bake in prepared bowls in heated oven for 20–

25 minutes or until the cakes test done. Cool them for 5 minutes in the bowls, then turn out onto a wire rack to cool completely.

Divide almond paste into 3 equal portions. Color 1 portion pink, another blue and leave third portion plain.

Brush the flat side of one cake with apricot jam glaze and set the flat side of the other cake on top. Trim the cake to a ball shape if necessary.

Roll out each portion of almond paste thinly on a board sprinkled with confectioners' sugar and cut 2 oval sections from each portion, cutting ends to a point. The best way to judge the right size is to measure the circumference of the ball with a piece of string. From point to point, each oval section should measure half of this circumference and the widest part only one-sixth of the circumference.

Brush 1 section of the cake 'ball' at a time with hot apricot jam glaze and press 1 of the 6 almond paste sections onto the cake so points just reach the top center and base of the cake.

Continue adding sections until the cake is completely covered, alternating the colors like a beach ball.

Smooth the seams of the ball with a metal spatula while the almond paste is still soft, then leave it to dry for 4–6 hours before serving.

Basket of Flowers

For light fruit cake
1 cup butter
1 cup dark brown sugar
grated rind of 1 lemon
5 eggs
2½ cups flour
1 teaspoon baking powder
pinch of salt
2 cups golden raisins
⅔ cup halved candied cherries
½ cup finely chopped mixed candied peel
½ cup shredded almonds
⅓ cup shelled pistachios, blanched and halved (optional)

To finish
¼ cup apricot jam glaze
1½ cup quantity of almond paste
royal icing, made with 3½ cups (1 lb) confectioners' sugar, 2 egg whites and 2 teaspoons lemon juice
1–2 squares (1–2 oz) semisweet chocolate
1–2 teaspoons instant coffee dissolved in a little water
marzipan roses (see page 81)
few fronds of maidenhair fern

8 inch springform pan; 8 inch circle of thin cardboard (for lid); 2 pastry bags or paper decorating cones; medium plain tube and shell tube for basket weave

This cake can be made 2–3 weeks ahead, stored in an airtight container and decorated when needed. Once decorated, it keeps well for 1–2 days if covered, but the fern must be added at the last minute.

Method
Set the oven at moderately low (325°F), line the cake pan with wax paper and grease it.

To make the cake: cream the butter, gradually add the sugar with the grated lemon rind and beat until the mixture is soft and fluffy. Beat in the eggs, one at a time, adding 1 tablespoon flour with each egg. Sift the remaining flour with the baking powder and salt and fold one-third into the egg mixture.

Toss the golden raisins, halved cherries, candied peel and nuts with a little of the remaining flour to coat them and stir into the cake batter. Fold in the remaining flour and spoon the mixture into the prepared pan. Bake in heated oven for 2¼–2½ hours or until a skewer inserted in the center comes out clean. If the cake is brown after 1½ hours' cooking, cover it with a sheet of foil.

Cool cake in the pan for 30 minutes, turn out onto a wire rack and cool completely. Store in an airtight container. If you moisten the cake with a little sherry or brandy from time to time during storage, the flavor will be improved.

To decorate: brush the cake with melted apricot jam glaze. Reserve about ½ cup of the almond paste, divide the remainder in half and roll one-half into a circle to cover the top of the cake. Roll out the second half into a long strip for the sides. Cover the cake with the paste and seal the edges.

Make the royal icing and keep it in a bowl covered with a damp cloth. Melt chocolate on a heatproof plate over a pan of hot water, cool it slightly and stir enough into about one-quarter of the royal icing to color it dark wicker brown. Stir enough instant coffee into the remaining icing to make it the color of straw. Cover the cake and cardboard lid with a lattice of icing (as shown at right).

Make the marzipan roses. Arrange them and maidenhair fern around top edge of half

the cake. Mound the reserved almond paste just behind the roses so that the lid can be propped open on it; tilt the lid on the cake so that the lowest edge joins the cake and the highest is above the roses to give the effect of a half-opened basket.

To make the 'basket' lid, put dark icing into a paper cone fitted with a medium plain tube and lighter icing into a cone fitted with shell tube. Mark the cardboard lid into 16 equal sections and pipe a line of dark icing from edge to center. Pipe straw-colored icing in a basket weave over it. Continue in this way until the whole lid is covered

After covering the cake with almond paste, cover the sides with a basket weave of royal icing. To keep it even, divide the sides vertically into 16 parts, using the lid as a guide

Marzipan for Decorations

4½ cups blanched, ground almonds
2 cups granulated sugar
1 cup water
2 egg whites, lightly beaten
juice of ½ lemon
1 teaspoon vanilla
3–4 tablespoons confectioners' sugar (for sprinkling)
few drops of red food coloring

Sugar thermometer; 1 inch plain cookie cutter or sharp bottle cap

This marzipan is almost white and so can be colored easily.

Method

In a saucepan heat sugar with water until dissolved. Bring to a boil and cook steadily until the syrup spins a thread when a little is lifted on a spoon (230°F–234°F on a sugar thermometer). Take pan from the heat and beat until syrup looks slightly cloudy. Stir in the ground almonds, add egg whites and cook over gentle heat for 2–3 minutes or until mixture pulls away from sides of the pan.

Add the lemon juice and vanilla and turn mixture onto a board sprinkled with confectioners' sugar. When the marzipan is cool, knead it until smooth.

To make Marzipan Roses

Carefully add red food coloring a few drops at a time, kneading the marzipan to distribute the coloring evenly – the roses should be deep pink. Roll out the marzipan thinly and cut it into circles with the cookie cutter or bottle cap. Make several cone-shaped bases and curl the circles around them to form petals. Use 2–3 petals for buds or 5–6 for larger roses.

Curl 'petals' of marzipan around the central base of rose. Use 2–3 petals for buds and 5–6 petals for roses; make about half a dozen of each

Steamship Birthday Cake

3-egg pound cake (see recipe for Battenburg cake on page 78)
2 cup quantity of almond paste (see page 78)
¾ cup apricot jam glaze (see page 78)
blue, green, red and yellow food coloring
few strands of spaghetti
royal icing, made with 3½ cups (1 lb) confectioners' sugar, 2 egg whites and 2 teaspoons lemon juice

Rectangular cake pan (11 X 7 inches)

Method

Set oven at moderate (350°F); grease and flour the cake pan, discarding the excess.

Make the cake batter and bake in the prepared pan for 25–30 minutes or until the cake tests done. Cool for 5 minutes in the pan, then turn out on a wire rack to cool completely.

Divide the almond paste in half and color one-half deep green with green and blue food coloring. Color the remaining almond paste a clear yellow with yellow coloring.

Trim the edges of the cake, cut it in half, lengthwise, brush one strip with apricot jam glaze and set the other on top. Trim one end to a point as the bows of the boat. Put the long sides of the 2 triangular-shaped trimmings together to form a rectangular 'cabin'.

On a board sprinkled with confectioners' sugar, roll out three-quarters of the yellow almond paste, cut a piece the same size as the boat and lay it on top of the cake. Cut small rounds from the remaining almond paste to form portholes. Brush one side of

the 'cabin' with apricot jam glaze and set it, glaze side down, on the almond paste deck. Brush the top and sides also with glaze.

Roll out two-thirds of the green almond paste to a long strip, trim the edges and press it around the sides of the boat. Roll out the remaining green almond paste and cover the cabin, smoothing the corners so there are no wrinkles. Brush the yellow almond paste portholes with apricot jam glaze and press them firmly around the sides of the boat. Color the remaining yellow almond paste bright orange with red and yellow food coloring, roll it out to a rectangle, trim the edges and twist it in a circle to form a funnel; set the funnel on the cabin.

Put a little royal icing into a paper decorating cone, snip off the tip and write the name of the boat on the bow or stern. Stick a short strand of spaghetti on a longer one with a dab of icing and stick this mast upright in front of the funnel. Set the cake on a tray or board covered with foil. Color the remaining royal icing turquoise blue with blue and green coloring and spread it around the cake, roughening it with a knife to resemble the sea; if you like, add a few trails of uncolored royal icing as white caps.

Never waste **leftover marzipan**. Add different flavorings and food coloring and shape it to resemble peaches, strawberries, oranges and other fruits which can be eaten as candies. Alternatively roll it into balls and sandwich it between 2 walnuts or use it to stuff pitted dessert dates (see marzipan candies in Volume 13).

Christmas chocolate log makes a festive centerpiece

Christmas Chocolate Log

For the chocolate roll
1 tablespoon dry cocoa
6 tablespoons flour
pinch of salt
4 eggs, separated
$\frac{1}{4}$ teaspoon cream of tartar
$\frac{3}{4}$ cup sugar
$\frac{1}{2}$ teaspoon vanilla

For meringue
1 egg white
$\frac{1}{4}$ cup granulated sugar
little confectioners' sugar
   (for sprinkling)
little grated chocolate

For decoration
1$\frac{1}{2}$ cup quantity of marzipan
   (see page 81)
little dissolved instant coffee
green food coloring
little confectioners' sugar
   (for sprinkling)

For chocolate butter cream
   frosting
3 squares (3 oz) semisweet
   chocolate
1 cup quantity of butter cream
   frosting (see page 24)

*15 X 10 inch jelly roll pan;
pastry bag; medium star
tube and $\frac{1}{4}$ inch plain tube*

This cake can be kept,
covered, for up to 48 hours.

Method

Set oven at moderately hot
(325°F) and grease and flour
the jelly roll pan.

   Sift flour several times with
the cocoa and salt. Beat egg
whites with the cream of tartar until they hold a stiff peak,
then gradually beat in half the
sugar. Continue beating until
the mixture is very glossy and
holds a peak again.

   Beat egg yolks until thick,
then gradually beat in the
remaining sugar with the
vanilla. Continue beating until

the mixture is thick and light
colored. With a metal spoon
carefully fold flour into the egg
yolk mixture alternately with
the egg whites until well
blended. Pour batter into the
prepared pan, spread evenly
and bake in heated oven for
20–25 minutes or until lightly
brown at the edges. Turn it
out, trim edges and roll it up
while still hot, with a dish
towel or sheet of wax paper
inside to prevent sticking.
Leave to cool.

   Make meringue and shape
into small 'mushrooms' (as in
tub of mushroom cake recipe,
page 84). Sprinkle them with
a little confectioners' sugar
and grated chocolate before
baking.

   For decoration: color two-
thirds of the marzipan with
instant coffee to a dark wood-
color. Roll into 2 long strips
and shape circles to form the
ends of the log and one or two
'knots' for the wood. Color the
remaining marzipan with green
coloring and roll it out thinly.
Cut out leaves and stems to
resemble a trail of ivy.

   For chocolate butter cream
frosting: melt chocolate on a
heatproof plate over a pan of
hot water and cool it. Make
butter cream frosting and beat
in the cool but still liquid
chocolate.

   To finish: unroll the chocolate roll, remove paper or
towel and spread roll with a
little chocolate butter cream
frosting. Then roll up again.
Spread the ends with a little
frosting and press the marzipan ends on the log. Put the
remaining frosting into a
pastry bag fitted with the star
tube and pipe lines along the
log to resemble bark, placing
the marzipan 'knots' here and
there along the log.

   Place a trail of marzipan ivy
along the log and arrange the
small meringue mushrooms
around the sides. Just before

serving, sprinkle it with confectioners' sugar to give the
effect of snow.

*Roll wood-colored marzipan
into long strips, then shape it
into 'knots' and ends for log.*

*Roll out the green-colored
marzipan and cut leaves and
stems for a trail of 'ivy'*

Tub of Mushroom Cake

For sponge cake
$\frac{3}{4}$ cup flour
pinch of salt
3 eggs
$\frac{1}{2}$ cup sugar

For French flan pastry
scant 1 cup flour
$\frac{1}{4}$ cup butter, softened
$\frac{1}{4}$ cup sugar
2 egg yolks
$\frac{1}{2}$ teaspoon vanilla

For meringue mushrooms
2 egg whites
$\frac{1}{2}$ cup sugar
little confectioners' sugar
(for sprinkling)
1 square (1 oz) semisweet
chocolate, finely grated

**For coffee butter cream
frosting**
2–3 teaspoons dry instant
coffee dissolved in a little
water
1 cup quantity of butter cream
frosting (see page 24)
1 teaspoon kirsch, or vanilla
14–16 ladyfingers

*8 inch springform pan; $\frac{1}{4}$ inch
plain tube; sugar
thermometer*

This cake will keep up to 24
hours in an airtight container.

Method

For cake: grease the pan and
sprinkle with sugar and flour.
Set oven at moderately hot
(375°F).

Sift the flour and salt 3–4
times. Put eggs in a bowl and
gradually beat in the sugar.

Set the bowl over a pan of
boiling water but not touch-
ing the water; take pan from
the heat. Beat sugar and eggs
for 10–12 minutes or until the
mixture is light and thick
enough to leave a ribbon trail
on itself when the beater is

lifted. Take the bowl off the
pan, and continue whisking 5
minutes or until the mixture is
cool. If using an electric
beater, no heat is necessary.

With a metal spoon, cut and
fold the flour into the mixture.
Pour batter into the prepared
pan and bake in heated oven
for 20–25 minutes or until the
cake tests done. Turn out and
cool it on a wire rack.

To make French flan pastry:
sift flour onto a board or
marble slab and make a well
in the center. Add butter,
sugar, egg yolks and vanilla
and work together with the
fingertips until smooth. Gradually draw in flour, working
with the whole hand to form a
smooth dough. Chill 30 minutes. Roll it out to a 10 inch
circle, place on a baking sheet,
prick with a fork, and bake in
a moderately hot oven (375°F)
for 12–15 minutes or until
lightly browned. Trim the
edges to a neat circle while
still warm and cool on a wire
rack.

To make meringue mush-
rooms: set the oven at low
(250°F) and beat egg whites
until they hold a stiff peak.
Add $1\frac{1}{2}$ tablespoons sugar and
continue beating until mixture
is stiff and glossy. Fold in
remaining sugar.

Fill pastry bag fitted with
the plain tube with meringue
and pipe out 'mushroom caps
and stems' in several sizes
onto a baking sheet lined with
silicone paper. Sprinkle the
caps lightly with confec-
tioners' sugar and grated
chocolate and bake in heated
oven for 30–40 minutes or
until stems are crisp and caps
are crisp on top. Lift stems
from paper and cool them.
Turn over caps, press in
underneath and bake 15 minutes longer or until dry.

Watchpoint: if the meringue
mushrooms start to brown
during baking, turn down the

heat.

Make butter cream frosting
and beat in the instant coffee
and kirsch or vanilla.

To assemble gâteau: set
the pastry circle on a cake
stand or plate. Split the
sponge cake in half and sandwich it with a little frosting.
Set it in the center of the
pastry circle, spread the top
and sides with frosting, reserving some for mushrooms, and
attach the ladyfingers to the
sides, trimming them to
resemble a tub. Set 2 long
ladyfingers on each side and
make a hole in the top of each
with a skewer to form the
characteristic tub side pieces.

With a small spatula fill the
indentations in the meringue
mushroom caps with remaining frosting and insert a
meringue mushroom stem.
Pile the meringue mushrooms
in the center, with 1–2 at the
side of the tub as if they had
fallen out. Chill at least 2
hours to allow the frosting to
mellow, then bring to room
temperature to serve.

*Use the butter cream frosting
to attach meringue mushroom
stems carefully to caps*

Ladyfingers

$\frac{1}{3}$ cup flour
pinch of salt
2 eggs, separated
1 extra egg white
$\frac{1}{3}$ cup sifted confectioners'
sugar
$\frac{1}{2}$ teaspoon vanilla
confectioners' sugar (for
sprinkling)

*Pastry bag and $\frac{1}{2}$ inch plain
tube, silicone paper
(optional)*

Makes 14–16 ladyfingers.

Method

Set oven at low (300°F).

Cover a baking sheet with
silicone paper, or grease it and
coat lightly with flour.

Sift flour and salt together
several times. Beat egg yolks
with an electric or rotary
beater until very thick and pale
in color. Beat egg whites until
they hold a stiff peak, then
gradually beat in sugar to
make a thick shiny meringue.
Add vanilla to yolks and beat
thoroughly, then fold in meringue. Add flour all at once and
fold in with a large metal
spoon.

Spoon batter carefully into
pastry bag fitted with the plain
tube and pipe fingers about
$3\frac{1}{2}$ inches long and 1 inch
apart on the prepared sheet.
Sprinkle the tops with confectioners' sugar and bake in
heated oven for 18–20 minutes or until pale beige in
color. Remove immediately
from the baking sheet and
cool on a wire rack.

Tub of mushrooms – pile meringue mushrooms on top and arrange a few at the side so they appear to have fallen out

COOKING WITH CHEESE

Be sure to use the right cheese for a recipe because this determines the flavor and texture of the finished dish. A strong cheese, for example, is needed to give character to a sauce, but a milder cheese is appropriate for fillings. Rich cheese with a high fat content is unsuitable for many dishes as the fat tends to separate. Cheese will form strings if it is overheated or cooked too long, and some types are more inclined to do so than others.

A good use for pieces of leftover cheese is to grate or crumble them and work them into cheese cream as a spread or make them into potted cheese.

KEY TO PHOTOGRAPH
1 French Gruyère (Beaufort).
2 Roquefort. 3 Tome au raisin.
4 Coeur. 5 Cendre d'olivet.
6 Langres. 7 Livarot. 8 Mimolette.
9 Pyramide. 10 Fromage au cumin. 11 Fromage au foin.

From the fresh cheeses that date from pre-Biblical times to the stronger hard cheeses, like Parmesan and Emmenthal, or veined varieties such as Roquefort and Gorgonzola, to the richest, most sophisticated triple crème — cheeses can satisfy the simplest or the most sophisticated tastes.

Before you buy at a cheese specialty shop, ask for sample bites. Or order cheese by mail through catalogues. But remember, there is no substitute for tasting.

Unfortunately in North America the word 'cheese' often means pre-packaged, **processed cheese**. Processed cheeses and cheese spreads, domestic and imported, are made by grinding, mixing and heating cheeses with an emulsifying agent and usually other chemicals. While convenient, they have a plastic quality, and never compare with natural cheeses.

Fresh Cheeses

The simplest natural preparation, **fresh cheese**, is made by placing coagulated milk in cheesecloth, hanging it up and leaving the whey to drain away until the curds are nearly solid. These are called **cream** or **pot cheese**; one variation is the fluffy, milk **cottage cheese**. All these cheeses should be stored for no longer than a few days.

Closely related are the drier, compact farmer cheeses that can be kept a little longer. Italian fresh cheeses include the mainstay of pizza, the soft and mild **Mozzarella** — tastiest when bought fresh at a local store in an Italian neighborhood — and the creamy **ricotta** with its bland almost sweet flavor that adapts well to sweet and savory foods; it is a favorite in pasta.

The fresh country cheeses of France are unsurpassed, but they are fragile and do not travel well. Those made with goat's and ewe's milk are more zesty than fresh cow's milk cheeses. There are many kinds and shapes (cylinders and cones are popular) and the names vary from region to region.

Many regions also make their own double and triple crème fresh cheeses such as **Boursault** and **Petit Suisse** that are available here. These rich and delicate cheeses are best at lunch or after a light dinner, eaten with fine sugar and strawberries or other fruits.

Hard Cheeses

Of the cheeses with pressed curds and a denser texture, **Cheddar** is the one that means cheese to most Americans. The original English Cheddar is still produced both in farmhouses and factories. Canadian Cheddar, made from unpasteurized milk, can be purchased at cheese specialty shops, and when aged it is almost like the English farmhouse variety.

Excellent American Cheddars are made in New York and Wisconsin. Other versions, such as **Colby** and **Longhorn**, are softer and more open in texture. When buying Cheddar from a wheel rather than already packaged, try to sample it first to taste for possible bitterness.

The closest, most outstanding relative of Cheddar is **Cheshire**, made in the county of Cheshire in England. Because of this cheese's saltiness, not always apparent at first, Cheshire is a good accompaniment to celery, radishes, cucumbers and vegetables that require additional salt.

The Cheddar group of cheeses, whose strong flavor has a natural affinity for beer, also includes **Caerphilly**, a compressed, white refreshing cheese that is good in hot weather and with salads; single and double **Gloucester**; **Leicester** — a bright orange-colored cheese with a creamy texture and a tangy aftertaste; white **Wensleydale**, another tangy cheese that is suitable to serve with cocktails, and **mimolette**, a French version with a brilliant orange color but, by Cheddar standards, mild in taste.

Blue-veined Cheeses

Among those cheeses whose curds are inoculated with a mold-producing substance, then left to ripen, is English **Stilton** which is generally regarded as one of the great cheeses of the world.

Unlike the French **Roquefort** made from sheep's milk and the softer Italian **Gorgonzola** — both ripened in cool caves — Stilton, made of the richest milk, is left to mature without refrigeration. Stilton's distinctive flavor, a blend of the blue-veined cheeses with hints of Cheddar, has traditionally led the English to eat it with crackers and port. It is also an ideal alternative to Cheddar with very tart apple pie for dessert.

Mild Cheeses

For those who prefer a blander cheese, there are many delightful varieties that serve as everyday staples. Italy's ivory-colored **Bel Paese** (also produced domestically) and semi-soft, buttery **Fontina**; France's creamy **Bonbel**, **Cœur** and **Reblochon**; America's **Muenster** and young **brick** cheese, popular in the west; Holland's ball-shaped, red-rinded **Edam** and whole-milk **Gouda**; Denmark's **Samso**, **Tybo** and **Danbo**; Norwegian **Tilsit** and **Jarlsberg** are some of the cheeses whose quality is dependable.

Often these mild cheeses are wrapped in a coating to add flavor — **tome au raisin**, covered in grape seeds, is particularly popular. Other examples are the French fresh country cheeses that are covered in grape leaves, cumin or caraway seeds and even wrapped in hay (**fromage** au foin) or the ashes of burned vine plants mixed with salt (cendre d'olivet).

Other creamy, richer cheeses devised by ingenious monks in the Middle Ages searching for a savory substitute for meat include robust **Port-Salut** and others with names like **St. Paulin** and **St. Remy**.

Soft Cheeses

France's most well-known cheese is the classic **Camembert**. This cheese is much better if it is not cut or packaged in triangles, since cutting the rind ends the normal aging process. Camemberts are also frequently overripe, so beware of cheeses that have shrunk inside their containers and those with pungent odors. A good Camembert should have a subtle, not strident flavor.

The sweet, rich **Brie** cheese with its satiny texture has been called the queen of cheeses.

Other similar cheeses are less well known, like the square **Pont l'Evêque** and the little **Livarot** from Normandy. To appreciate the flavor of all these cheeses it is important to catch their peak of ripeness when the texture is soft and glistening throughout, neither oozing, nor with a hard, unripe layer in the center. The flavor should be rich and mellow with no trace of the pungent ammonia that develops when the cheese is overripe.

Crema Danica, the Danish version of these cheeses invented in 1957, is more delicate than Camembert. It has the additional advantage of ripening quickly and smoothly so that quality is more consistent, although it,

too, can become pungent when overripe.

Cooking and Table Cheeses

Hearty cheeses like Cheddar, **Swiss Emmenthal** and **Gruyère** are best for snacks or served with a meal. Emmenthal and Gruyère are often thought of as cooking cheeses but they are excellent table cheeses too. While they share a sweet and mellow flavor, their differences go farther than just the relative size of their holes.

The larger eyes in Swiss Emmenthal, formed by acid bacteria, result from fermentation in a warm, humid cellar at a constant temperature. The cheese then matures for 4 months or longer.

Swiss Gruyère, which produces smaller eyes, is cured for a longer period of time in a cellar where the temperature varies. The rind is not dry, like Emmenthal, but wrinkled and somewhat greasy.

Gruyère has a rich mild flavor but is more likely than Parmesan to form strings when overheated, particularly if it is not well aged and dry. In recipes throughout these Volumes, unless otherwise specified, you can use the true Swiss Gruyère (with small holes) or the French and American Gruyère (with large holes).

The **French Gruyère**, sometimes called **Beaufort**, is not as sweet as the Swiss and has a little more tang.

Processed versions of these two cheeses – some with ham, wine and spices added – are designed to keep longer, so note what you are buying. Also make sure that you are buying Swiss or French

Gruyère or Emmenthal – their imitations tend to be rubbery.

True Italian **Parmesan**, delicately grained and subtly flavored, is one of the best cooking and table cheeses. It has the unique characteristic of bringing out other flavors and is particularly good in cooking because it does not become stringy when heated. Parmesan is a solid, close-textured cheese so that even when it is finely grated, you can taste the remarkable flavor.

It should be mixed with a mild rich cheese (ideally Gruyère or Emmenthal or a mature dry Cheddar) for use in soufflés and sauces. It is also good for sprinkling on top of a dish as it browns quickly and well.

Parmesan is generally available already grated in packages, but the flavor is fresher and more pungent if the cheese is grated just before use. Many specialty markets carry Parmesan both freshly grated and in the piece.

Romano and **Pecorino** cheese are good substitutes for Parmesan – they are less expensive but have a harsher flavor.

How to Serve Cheese

When serving cheeses, whether as hors d'œuvre, entrée or end of the meal, bring out the full flavor by serving them at room temperature. (It usually takes 1–3 hours for cheese to reach its best after being taken from the refrigerator.) Serve at least three different kinds of cheese, including one hard, one soft and one fresh country cheese like Petit Suisse or a goat cheese. Display the cheeses on natural wood or mats – just as they are kept while curing.

Cut only as much as you expect to use so you do not have any leftovers; you can always replenish with a fresh piece. Do not place mild cheeses next to strong ones, or they will lose their subtle flavor.

Red wine is generally regarded as the perfect foil for all cheeses, but chilled white wines also go well with delicate cheeses like Bel Paese, and a hearty beer or ale complements strong cheeses like **Limburger**, **Liederkranz** and **European Muenster**. It is interesting to serve regional cheese with native dishes – salty Greek **feta** with moussaka or a moist Parmesan following an Italian meal.

Cheese pancakes are a delicious way of combining cheese and beer or ale

Cheese Pancakes

1½ cups flour
1 teaspoon salt
1 teaspoon baking powder
3 eggs, beaten to mix
3 tablespoons melted butter
¾ cup beer or ale
½–¾ cup milk
butter (for frying)

For cheese mixture
1½ cups grated sharp Cheddar
    cheese
2 tablespoons butter
¼ cup beer or ale
1½ teaspoons prepared
    mustard
pinch of cayenne

6–7 inch skillet or frying pan

Makes 12–14 pancakes.

Method
To make the pancakes: sift the flour with the salt and baking powder into a bowl, make a well in the center and add the eggs, melted butter, beer or ale and half the milk. Stir until the batter is just mixed, cover, and let stand 1–2 hours. If the batter is too thick to pour easily, add the remaining milk.

In the skillet melt a little butter and, when foaming, pour in enough batter to cover the bottom of the pan. Cook over medium heat until bubbles rise to the surface of the pancake and the underside is browned. Turn it and brown the other side. Turn out the pancake onto a plate and fry the remaining pancakes in the same way, piling them one on top of another to keep warm.

To make the cheese mixture: in the top of a double boiler melt the butter, add the cheese and melt it slowly over hot but not boiling water, stirring occasionally. Do not allow it to get too hot. Gradually stir in the beer or ale and seasonings.

When creamy, sandwich the pancakes with the cheese mixture, piling them one on top of another in 2–3 stacks on heatproof dishes. Pour the remaining mixture on top, brown the pancakes under the broiler and serve at once, cut into wedges like a cake.

Celery Pinwheels

bunch of celery
2 tablespoons butter
1 package (3 oz) cream cheese
1 package Liederkrantz cheese
    or 3–4 wedges of Camembert
    cheese (without rind)
10–12 buttered slices of
    wholewheat bread
1–2 slices of canned pimiento
    (for garnish)

Method
Separate the celery stalks, wash thoroughly and dry.

Cream the butter and beat in the cream cheese. Beat the Liederkrantz or Camembert into the cream cheese mixture.

Fill each stalk of celery with the cheese mixture and, starting with the smallest pieces, reshape the bunch. Wrap tightly in wax paper and chill. When firmly set, cut in slices.

With a cookie cutter, cut the wholewheat bread in circles the same diameter as the celery, place the celery slices on the bread and garnish with a strip of pimiento curved into a circle.

Cold Cheese Soufflé

¾ cup grated Parmesan or dry
    Cheddar cheese
1½ cups béchamel sauce,
    made with 2 tablespoons
    butter, 2 tablespoons flour
    and 1½ cups milk (infused
    with a bay leaf, a slice of
    onion, 6 peppercorns and a
    blade of mace)
2 egg yolks
1 teaspoon Dijon-style mustard
salt and pepper
1 envelope gelatin
¼ cup stock or water
squeeze of lemon juice
½ cup heavy cream, whipped
    until it holds a soft shape
3 egg whites

For garnish
bunch of watercress
2–3 tomatoes, sliced
2–3 tablespoons grated
    Parmesan cheese

Soufflé dish (1 quart capacity)

Method
Circle a strip of wax paper or foil around soufflé dish so it is 1½ inches higher than the dish; tie with string to make a stand-up collar. Stand an oiled bottle (1 cup capacity) in the center of the dish.

Make béchamel sauce, cool it slightly, then beat in egg yolks, cheese, mustard and plenty of seasoning.

Sprinkle gelatin over the stock or water, let stand 5 minutes until spongy and dissolve over a pan of hot water. Stir into cheese mixture with the lemon juice. Chill, stirring occasionally. Beat the egg whites until they hold a soft shape. When the mixture starts to set, fold in the whipped cream, then the egg whites. Pour the mixture into the prepared soufflé dish – it should rise at least 1 inch above level of dish. Chill at least 2 hours or until set.

Just before serving, carefully remove paper collar and bottle from the center of soufflé and fill the cavity with watercress. Garnish the top with slices of tomato and press grated Parmesan around the sides.

Watchpoint: the cheese for the soufflé must be dry and full of flavor. If using Cheddar, it is better to mix it with some Parmesan, otherwise the soufflé will be too bland.

Potted Cheese

1½ cups grated or crumbled
    mixed cheeses, including a
    little Roquefort or any other
    blue cheese
6 tablespoons butter
2–3 tablespoons port or sherry
salt and pepper

*Small china or earthenware
pots*

Method
Cream the butter and gradually work in the cheeses. When the mixture becomes stiff, add the port or sherry. Season well.

Press the cheese into the small pots and smooth the tops. If not using immediately, cover each pot with foil and, if possible, a lid. Store in a cool place for up to 3 weeks.

Serve the cheese in pots or turn it out and cut into wedges.

Tiropetes
(Greek Cheese Pastries)

1 package (½ lb) phyllo pastry
    sheets (available at Greek
    stores and delicatessens)
½ cup melted butter

For filling
¾ lb feta cheese, crumbled
2 eggs, beaten to mix
½ teaspoon black pepper

Makes about 48 pastries.

Method
Work cheese through a sieve
and beat in the eggs with the
pepper to make a smooth
mixture. Set oven at hot
(425°F).

Unwrap the pastry sheets
and cut them into 2 inch strips.
Watchpoint: phyllo pastry
sheets are hard to handle as
they are paper thin and dry
quickly — use them a few
sheets at a time and keep the
remainder covered with a
damp cloth while working.

Brush a strip with melted
butter and put a teaspoon of
filling at one end. Fold a
corner of the pastry sheet over
the top of the mixture to meet
the other side. Continue
folding the sheet over and
over to form a small triangle
with the filling wrapped inside.
Brush with melted butter and
place on a baking sheet. Use
remaining filling and pastry
sheets in the same way.

Bake tiropetes in heated
oven for 15 minutes or until
they are puffed and golden.
Serve hot or cold as hors
d'œuvre. Tiropetes freeze well
and can be baked as needed.

Austrian Cheese Pastries

¾ cup grated dry Cheddar
    cheese
1½ cups flour
½ cup butter
½ cup ground blanched almonds
salt and pepper
1 egg yolk
2 teaspoons water (optional)
1 egg, beaten, to mix
Parmesan cheese (for
    sprinkling)

For filling
3 tablespoons grated Cheddar
    or Gruyère cheese
¾ cup milk
1 teaspoon arrowroot
salt and pepper
1 teaspoon paprika
1 egg, separated

1–1½ inch round cookie cutter

Makes about 35 pastries (1½
inch size).

Method
Sift flour into a bowl and rub
in the butter lightly with the
fingertips. Add ground
almonds, cheese and sea-
soning and work in the egg
yolk, with water if necessary,
to make a smooth dough. Chill
the dough at least 30 minutes.

Set oven at moderately hot
(375°F).

Roll out dough to about
one-eighth inch thickness and
cut into 1–1½ inch circles.
Brush half of these with
beaten egg and sprinkle them
with grated Parmesan cheese.
Leave the other half plain.
Place the rounds on baking
sheets and bake in heated
oven for 10–12 minutes or
until they are golden brown.
Cool them slightly, then lift
onto a wire rack.

To make the filling: mix
all the ingredients together
including the egg yolk but set
the egg white aside. Bring the
mixture slowly to a boil, stirring, and remove from the
heat as soon as it boils. Beat
the egg white until it holds a
soft shape and fold into the
hot mixture. Bring just back to
a boil and cool.

Sandwich the rounds with
a generous teaspoon of the
filling, using the plain round
as the base.

These cheese pastries can
be made in much larger sizes
and served for lunch with a
green salad.

Cheese Cream

1½ cups grated mixed hard
    cheeses or sharp Cheddar
6 tablespoons butter
1 cup hot milk
1–2 tablespoons chopped
    mixed herbs (chives, parsley,
    thyme, basil) – optional
salt and pepper

Method
Cream the butter and gradually work in the cheeses.
When the mixture thickens,
add the hot milk and con-
tinue beating until it is light
and creamy. Add herbs to
taste or leave plain.

Season well with salt and
plenty of pepper. Serve with
fingers of toast or as a sandwich filling.

Roquefort Mousse

¼ lb Roquefort cheese
1 envelope gelatin
3 tablespoons lemon juice
¾ cup hot water
1 cup grated cucumber,
    drained
3 tablespoons chopped parsley
2 tablespoons chopped red
    bell pepper, blanched
1 teaspoon chopped onion
1 teaspoon salt
black pepper, freshly ground
1 cup heavy cream, whipped
    until it holds a soft shape
watercress (for garnish)

Ring mold (1½ quart capacity)

Method
Sprinkle gelatin over the
lemon juice, let stand 5 minutes until spongy, then add
hot water and stir until
dissolved.

Crush or mash the cheese
and mix with the cucumber,
parsley, red pepper and onion.
Add seasoning and stir in
gelatin. Stand in a pan of
water with ice cubes and
chill, stirring occasionally,
until the mixture begins to
thicken. Fold in the cream,
spoon the mixture into the
mold and chill for at least 2
hours or until firm.

Just before serving, turn
the mousse out onto a platter;
garnish the center with watercress. Serve as an appetizer
or for lunch.

Homemade cheese cream, flavored with fresh herbs, is served with fingers of toast

A selection of cheeses, from left to right, top: Mozzarella, Swiss Emmenthal, Cheddar, Parmesan, two potted cheeses and some grated Parmesan

Swiss Cheese Fondue

2–2½ cups (10–12 oz) grated
   Swiss Emmenthal cheese
2–2½ cups (10–12 oz) grated
   Swiss Gruyère cheese
1 clove of garlic, cut in half
1 tablespoon flour
1 cup dry white wine
1 teaspoon lemon juice
3 tablespoons kirsch
¼ teaspoon ground nutmeg
black pepper, freshly ground
French bread (for serving)

*Fondue pot or heavy pan;
portable burner*

Method
Rub inside the pot with garlic. Toss cheeses with flour. Combine in pan with wine and lemon juice and bring to a boil over moderate heat, stirring constantly in a figure eight pattern.
Watchpoint: the fondue will separate if stirred too fast or heated too quickly but, at the same time, you must be careful not to cook it too slowly or it will separate when the cheese melts.

Add kirsch and nutmeg and season with plenty of pepper. Bring the mixture just back to a boil. It should be creamy in consistency and is ready to serve at this point. Keep it simmering throughout the meal and serve with French bread cut into cubes. The brown crust left on the bottom of the fondue pot is regarded as a great delicacy.

The **original Swiss cheese fondue** was described in 1825 by the gastronome Brillat-Savarin as being made of buttered eggs with cheese. Today there are many fondue recipes, and most include Gruyère and Emmenthal cheeses.

A combination of cheeses is used because a fondue made with Gruyère alone becomes stringy quickly unless great care is taken. Parmesan adds a distinctive flavor.

For a fondue party, a special fondue pot is placed on a portable burner in the center of the table (any shallow heavy pan or flameproof dish may be used instead). Guests dip crusts of French bread or toast into the fondue using long-handled forks.

Simple Fondue

6 eggs, beaten to mix
½ cup butter
1 cup (½ lb) grated Gruyère
   cheese
1 cup (½ lb) grated Cheddar
   cheese
½ cup (¼ lb) freshly grated
   Parmesan cheese
3–4 tablespoons dry white wine
   or heavy cream
salt and pepper
toast or French bread (for
   serving)

*Fondue pot or heavy pan;
portable burner*

Method
Pour the beaten eggs into the pot and set over very low heat, stirring constantly. When the eggs are just beginning to set, add the butter in small pieces and, when melted, gradually add the cheese and wine or cream. Season and continue stirring until the mixture is thick and creamy.

Serve with toast or French bread as for Swiss cheese fondue.

Tomatoes Stuffed with Roquefort Cream

8 even-sized medium tomatoes
¼ lb Roquefort or any other
   blue cheese
salt and pepper
2 hard-cooked eggs
3 stalks of celery (preferably
   from center of bunch),
   finely diced
2 tablespoons heavy cream
¼ cup vinaigrette dressing
   (see page 63)
1 teaspoon chopped chives

Method
Scald and peel tomatoes. Cut a thin slice from the bottom (not stalk end) of each one for a lid, and carefully scoop out the seeds and core with a teaspoon. Drain and season the insides.

Chop the whites of the hard-cooked eggs and mix with the celery. Sieve the cheese and beat half with the cream until smooth. Stir in the celery and egg mixture and spoon into the tomatoes, mounding the mixture. Replace the lids of the tomatoes on a slant.

Beat the vinaigrette dressing into the remaining cheese and add the chives.

Work the egg yolks through a sieve onto a platter, arrange the tomatoes on top and spoon over the cheese dressing.

Roquefort and Walnut Salad

¼ cup crushed Roquefort or
  any blue cheese
12 walnut halves
2 heads of Bibb lettuce or the
  hearts of 2 firm Boston
  lettuce
3 slices of white bread
½ cup vinaigrette dressing (see
  page 63)

Method
Wash and dry the lettuce and chill until crisp. Cut the crusts from the bread and toast the slices until golden. When cold cut each slice into four and spread with crushed Roquefort.

Just before serving toss the lettuce in a bowl with walnuts, Roquefort toasts and vinaigrette dressing.

Roquefort Salad

8–10 slices of bacon
1¼–1½ lb small new potatoes
salt and pepper

For dressing
½ cup Roquefort cheese
½ cup vinaigrette dressing (see
  page 63)
¾ cup heavy cream
watercress (for garnish)

Method
Dice the bacon, fry until crisp and drain. Boil the potatoes in their skins until tender; drain and peel while hot. Slice them and moisten with vinaigrette dressing. Add fried bacon and season to taste.

For dressing: crush or mash the Roquefort well and beat in the remaining vinaigrette dressing with the cream; season to taste if needed. Pile the potatoes in a bowl and spoon over the dressing. Garnish with watercress.

Avocado Stuffed with Cheese

3 avocados
2 small packages (3 oz each)
  cream cheese
1–2 teaspoons anchovy paste
6 ripe olives, pitted and
  chopped
juice of 1 lemon
lettuce leaves (for garnish) –
  optional
½ cup vinaigrette dressing
  (see page 63)
toasted croûtes of bread
  (for canapés) – optional

Serve as an hors d'œuvre or appetizer.

Method
Work cream cheese until soft and beat in anchovy paste and olives. Halve avocados lengthwise and discard the seeds; peel the avocados. Fill the cavities with cream cheese mixture and reshape avocados. Roll them completely in lemon juice, wrap in plastic wrap and chill.

To serve as an hors d'œuvre: again slice the reshaped avocados crosswise, but crush the end slices which contain no cheese. Spread the pulp on toasted croûtes of bread and set a slice of cheese-stuffed avocado on top and brush with vinaigrette dressing.

To serve as an appetizer: cut reshaped avocados into slices crosswise and arrange on lettuce leaves on individual dishes, spoon over vinaigrette dressing just before serving.

Make and serve the same day.

Gannat
(Cheese Bread)

1 cup grated Gruyère,
  Emmenthal or Cheddar
  cheese
2 cups flour, sifted with
  ¼ teaspoon salt and pinch of
  pepper
½ cup milk
¼ cup butter
1 package dry yeast or
  1 cake of compressed yeast
1 teaspoon sugar
2 eggs

*7 inch springform pan or large
loaf pan*

This rich cheese bread makes delicious sandwiches or can be served with butter as an appetizer accompaniment.

Method
Put flour into a warm bowl and make a well in the center. Warm the milk with the butter until melted and pour into the well. The milk mixture should be lukewarm in temperature. Sprinkle over the yeast, add the sugar and leave 5 minutes or until the yeast has dissolved. Beat the eggs to a froth, add to the yeast mixture and stir, gradually drawing in the flour to form a soft dough. Knead on a lightly floured board for 5 minutes until the mixture is smooth and elastic, cover the bowl and leave in a warm place for 1 hour or until the dough has doubled in bulk. Work in the cheese, reserving 1 tablespoon.

Set oven at hot (400°F) and grease the springform or loaf pan.

Transfer dough to the pan, cover and leave in a warm place for about 30 minutes to rise again until double in bulk. Sprinkle with the remaining cheese and bake in heated oven for 35–45 minutes, or until bread is brown and sounds hollow when tapped on the bottom. When baked in a springform pan, the bread may be split and sandwiched with cheese cream (see page 92), if you like.

Toasted Cheese

4–6 oz dry Cheddar cheese
½ teaspoon prepared mustard
black pepper, freshly ground
2–3 tablespoons ale
4–6 slices of freshly toasted
  bread

Method
Slice the cheese thinly and lay in a baking dish. Spread the mustard over the cheese and add plenty of pepper. Pour on the ale, cover and set the dish in a water bath over low heat until the cheese begins to melt.

Take from the heat, stir carefully, then put back over the heat until all the cheese has melted. Serve at once, with hot dry toast.

Gannat (cheese bread) makes delicious sandwiches or can be served as an appetizer accompaniment

For an easy supper dish, make individual ramekins au fromage

Ramekins au Fromage
(Cheese Ramekins)

½ cup grated Cheddar cheese
2 eggs
1½ cups milk
salt and pepper
2 slices of stale bread,
    crusts removed and diced
    (for croûtons)
¼ cup butter
8 anchovy fillets
½ teaspoon paprika

*6–8 ramekins or individual
    soufflé dishes*

Method
Set oven at moderately hot
(375°F).
    Beat the eggs until smooth
and stir in the milk and
cheese. Season to taste.
    Fry bread in 3 tablespoons
butter until golden. Drain the
croûtons on paper towels.
    Divide each anchovy in 2–3
pieces.
    Butter the ramekins, put a
spoonful of the croûtons and
a few pieces of anchovy in
each one and fill with the egg
mixture. Bake in a water bath
in heated oven for 15–20
minutes or until the ramekins
are golden and firm to the
touch. Sprinkle with paprika
and serve.

Welsh Rarebit

1 cup grated sharp Cheddar
    cheese
1½ tablespoons butter
2 tablespoons ale or milk
1 teaspoon prepared mustard
pinch of cayenne
4–6 slices of hot buttered toast

Method
In the top of a double boiler
melt the butter, add the
cheese and melt it slowly over
hot but not boiling water,

stirring occasionally. Do not
allow it to get too hot.
    Gradually stir in the ale or
milk and seasonings. When
creamy, spoon the mixture
onto the slices of buttered
toast. Brown quickly under the
broiler, if you like, and serve
the rarebit very hot.

Croque Monsieur

For 1 serving
1 square slice of ham
2 square slices of Gruyère
    cheese
2 slices of white bread
2 tablespoons butter (optional)

Croque monsieur is a popular
French snack served in most
cafés and bistros. Croque
madame is less well known.

Method
Sandwich the ham between
cheese slices and place inside
the slices of bread. Trim off
the crusts and toast the sandwich under the broiler until
the cheese is melted and
bread is golden on both sides.

If you prefer, the sandwich
can be fried in butter. Leave
whole if serving as a snack or
cut in four for cocktail hors
d'œuvre.

Croque Madame

For 1 serving
½ cup cooked chicken, cut in
    strips
2 square slices of Gruyère
    cheese
2 slices of white bread
2 tablespoons butter (optional)

Method
Prepare and cook as for
croque monsieur, spreading
the chicken between the
slices of cheese.

Omelet Barante, with lobster and mushroom filling, is decorated with the halved lobster shell

SOPHISTICATED QUICK DISHES

To celebrate a special occasion with a minimum of effort but with maximum results, try making one of the following quick recipes. They are superb but extravagant because, with a few exceptions such as plain omelets and hamburgers, most quick recipes call for luxury ingredients like steak and seafood.

To make an Omelet

Use a 9–10 inch pan for an 8-egg omelet to serve 4.

Beat eggs in a bowl with a fork until frothy and add water and seasoning. Heat pan over medium heat, add butter in 2 pieces, and as soon as it is foaming pour in the egg mixture. Leave 10–15 seconds before stirring around slowly with the flat of a fork. Stir once or twice around pan, then cook for 5–6 seconds longer.

Lift up edge of omelet to let any remaining uncooked egg run on to the hot pan. (Some people prefer omelets that are soft in the center, others prefer them cooked through, so the length of cooking time depends on individual preference.) Add any filling.

Tilt the pan away from you and fold omelet over to the far side. Change your grip on the pan so the handle runs up the palm of your hand. Hold a warm platter with your other hand, tilt platter slightly and turn omelet out onto it.

Omelet Barante

8 eggs
1 small (1–1¼ lb) cooked lobster
1½ cups mornay sauce, made with 2 tablespoons butter, 2 tablespoons flour, 1½ cups milk (infused with slice of onion, 6 peppercorns, blade of mace and bay leaf), ¼ cup grated Parmesan cheese, ½ teaspoon Dijon-style mustard
2 cups (½ lb) sliced mushrooms
6–7 tablespoons butter
salt and pepper
6 tablespoons port
½ cup heavy cream
2 tablespoons water
¼ cup grated Parmesan cheese (for sprinkling)

This delicious omelet was dedicated to the Baron de Barante, a famous 19th century gourmet and historian. It was also King Edward VII of England's favorite omelet.

Method
Cut lobster in half lengthwise and remove the meat, discarding intestinal tract and head sac. Cut meat in slices. Crack claws and remove meat from them and the legs. Reserve lobster shell and oil it lightly for decoration.

Make the mornay sauce and keep warm.

Sauté the mushrooms in half the butter until tender, season lightly, add port and simmer until reduced by half. Take from heat, stir in the cream, add lobster meat, cover and simmer 4–5 minutes. Keep warm.

Beat the eggs lightly with the water and seasoning. Make the omelet, using the rest of the butter. While it is still soft and creamy in the middle, spoon in the lobster mixture, then fold over and turn onto a heatproof platter.

Coat at once with mornay sauce, sprinkle generously with grated cheese and brown under the broiler.

Garnish the platter with the halved lobster shell and serve at once.

Spoon the mushroom and lobster mixture into omelet while it is still soft and fold over

Germiny refers to dishes — usually soups or omelets — that contain sorrel. This tart, dark green-leaved vegetable is occasionally available in the spring in specialty markets. Arugla is a good substitute if you can find it, otherwise use Bibb or romaine lettuce. Treat arugla like sorrel but do not blanch lettuce.

Omelet Germiny

8 eggs
1 cup sorrel leaves
2 cups spinach leaves
1½ cups mornay sauce (as for omelet Barante)
8–10 scallions
5–6 tablespoons butter
salt and pepper
½ cup heavy cream
2 tablespoons water
¼ cup grated Gruyère cheese (for sprinkling)

Method
Prepare mornay sauce; keep warm. Trim the scallions, leaving on 1–2 inches of green tops, and blanch 5–6 minutes. Drain, return to the pan with 1 tablespoon butter and sauté 2–3 minutes or until very soft but not brown. Keep warm.

Wash the sorrel and spinach leaves thoroughly and blanch them together in boiling water for 1 minute. Drain, press between 2 plates to remove excess water and chop leaves.

In a pan melt 2 tablespoons butter, add spinach and sorrel, season, cover and cook gently for 4–5 minutes. Take off the lid, increase the heat to evaporate any moisture, add the cream and simmer, uncovered, for 2–3 minutes. Keep warm.

Beat the eggs lightly with the water and seasoning. Make the omelet, using the rest of the butter, and when set but still soft and creamy in the middle spread the spinach mixture on top. Fold over the omelet and turn onto a heatproof platter. Coat with mornay sauce, sprinkle with grated cheese and brown under the broiler.

Garnish with scallions and serve at once.

Smoked Trout in Parsley Aspic

4 smoked trout
1 lemon, sliced (for decoration)
1 tablespoon chopped parsley
(for sprinkling)
2 slices onion, pushed into
rings

For parsley aspic
$\frac{1}{4}$ cup chopped parsley
2 cups white wine
2 cups veal or chicken stock
2 teaspoons tarragon or white
wine vinegar
1 envelope gelatin
salt and pepper

Smoked trout in parsley aspic are decorated with circles of lemon

Method
Remove the skin from the trout, leaving the head and tail. Snip the backbone at each end and pull it out carefully to the side so that the meat is left intact. Lay the trout in a deep serving dish and chill them.

To make the parsley aspic: simmer the wine until it is reduced by half. Add the stock, reserving $\frac{1}{4}$ cup, and the vinegar and continue simmering for 5 minutes. Sprinkle the gelatin over the reserved stock, let stand 5 minutes until it is spongy and stir into the hot wine mixture until dissolved. Let cool to tepid, add the parsley and taste for seasoning.

Pour the aspic into the dish of trout — it should almost cover them. Cover and chill 2 hours or until set — the aspic should not be too firm.

Sprinkle with chopped parsley and decorate with circles of lemon and onion just before serving.

Steak tartare is served individually with a garnish of chopped egg white, gherkin pickles, shallots and capers

Steak Tartare

1½–2 lb very lean ground steak
1½ teaspoons salt
1 teaspoon freshly ground
   black pepper
3 tablespoons oil
1 tablespoon wine vinegar
1 teaspoon prepared or
   Dijon-style mustard
dash of Tabasco
4 shallots, finely chopped
4 gherkin pickles, finely
   chopped
2 tablespoons chopped capers
4 egg yolks

For garnish (optional)
2 hard-cooked eggs
½ onion, sliced and pushed into
   rings
2 gherkin pickles, sliced
1 tablespoon chopped parsley

The basic ingredients of steak tartare are always the same — very lean ground steak, egg yolks and a variety of seasonings which must be carefully balanced. The flavor depends very much on the freshness and quality of the meat. Allow ⅓–½ lb steak per person; opinions vary on which is the best cut to use — fillet, round or chuck.

Method

Put the ground steak in a large bowl with salt and pepper. Work together well with oil, vinegar, mustard and Tabasco, then add the shallots, gherkins and capers. When thoroughly mixed, add the egg yolks, mix again and taste for seasoning.

To serve on a platter: mound steak on the platter. Cut hard-cooked eggs in half, finely chop egg whites and work yolks through a sieve. Garnish the platter with onion rings, gherkin slices, egg white and yolk and chopped parsley. Serve with French, pumpernickel or rye bread.

To serve individually (as photographed): mound a portion of unseasoned ground steak on each plate, make a hollow in the center and add 1 egg yolk. Garnish with chopped shallots, gherkin pickles, capers and hard-cooked egg white, leaving each person to mix the steak with egg yolk, garnishes, seasoning, oil, vinegar, mustard and Tabasco, according to taste. Sprinkle with parsley and sieved egg yolk before eating.

Grind the beef steak very finely to make steak tartare

Place a raw egg yolk in the center of the mounded steak

Emincés de Veau Hongroise

1½ lb veal escalopes, cut about
   ¼ inch thick
3 tablespoons butter
2 teaspoons paprika
1 tablespoon flour
¾ cup well-flavored chicken
   or veal stock
¾ cup heavy cream
salt and pepper

For fresh tomato purée
3 tomatoes, peeled, seeded
   and chopped
2 tablespoons butter
pinch of sugar

'Emincer' is a French cooking term meaning to slice thinly (meat, vegetables or fruit).

Method

To make tomato purée: melt butter in a saucepan, add tomatoes with sugar and seasoning and simmer gently, stirring occasionally, for 10–15 minutes or until mixture is thick and concentrated.

If necessary, trim any skin and membrane from veal; cut it in thin strips. Sauté quickly in the butter over high heat just until it begins to brown.

Stir in the paprika and flour, add the fresh tomato purée and stock and bring to a boil, stirring. Simmer, uncovered, for 10 minutes or until the veal is very tender, stirring occasionally. Add the cream, bring to a boil, taste for seasoning and simmer gently for 5 minutes or until sauce is creamy and fairly thick. Serve with boiled rice.

Veal Escalopes Tapenade

4–8 veal escalopes (about 1½ lb)
¼ cup butter
salt and pepper
¾ cup ripe olives, pitted and
   shredded
½ cup white wine
pinch of sugar
grated rind and juice of ½ lemon
1½ teaspoons tomato paste

This is a simple Mediterranean dish, but like many simple dishes, top quality ingredients are essential; the veal must be of prime quality and the olives should be strong-flavored Greek-style olives.

Strickly speaking, a tapenade is a paste made of black olives pounded with oil and anchovy which is spread on partly cooked veal escalopes; then they are coated with egg and crumbs and fried. However, this version is easier and equally good.

Method

If necessary, trim any skin and membrane from escalopes and then place them between 2 sheets of wax paper and pound until very thin and flat.

In a skillet melt the butter, brown the escalopes on both sides, season them, cover pan and cook gently for 15 minutes. Add olives and cook 10 minutes longer. Transfer escalopes and olives to a platter and keep warm.

Add wine to the pan, season and add the sugar. Boil 10 seconds, stir in the lemon rind and juice and tomato paste. Spoon this sauce over the escalopes and serve immediately.

Tournedos Rossini

4–6 tournedos steaks, cut 1½–2 inches thick (1½–2 lb)
4–6 slices of bread (for croûtes)
4–6 tablespoons clarified butter (for frying)
4–6 slices of foie gras, or other creamy liver pâté
2 teaspoons chopped canned truffles or 1 canned truffle (drained and cut in 4–6 thick slices)
bunch of watercress (for garnish)

For Madeira sauce
2 cups espagnole sauce (see Volume 2)
¼ cup sherry or Madeira
salt and pepper

This classic dish was named for the composer Rossini. The tournedos, which are thickly cut steaks from the fillet, are pan fried, topped with a slice of foie gras or pâté and served with Madeira sauce.

Method
Cut croûtes from the bread the same size as the tournedos and fry in half the butter until golden. Drain well. Put the foie gras or pâté slices on a buttered ovenproof dish, cover with buttered foil and heat about 10 minutes in a very low oven (200°F–250°F).

Mix the espagnole sauce with the sherry or Madeira in a pan, season highly and simmer, uncovered, for 10–15 minutes.

Meanwhile, pan fry the tournedos in remaining butter in a heavy skillet or frying pan over high heat for 3–4 minutes on each side for rare steak, 5 minutes on each side for medium done steak, turning them once and seasoning after turning.

Set each tournedos on a

Tournedos Rossini are topped with foie gras and truffle and served with Madeira sauce

croûte, arrange on a platter and lay a slice of foie gras or pâté on each one. Top with a slice of truffle or add chopped truffles with their liquid to the Madeira sauce and spoon a little over the tournedos to coat them and the center of the platter. Garnish with watercress and serve remaining sauce separately.

Foie gras is the liver of a goose that has been specially fattened and is a great delicacy. The liver is usually cooked in a pâté flavored with truffles and, when cut, it is firm, yet creamy. When used in a hot dish, it does not disintegrate as other liver pâtés are inclined to do.

Foie gras is available here in cans and jars and it is almost as expensive as truffles. Other creamy liver pâté can be used instead — if possible it should be made of chicken or duck livers.

Suprêmes of Chicken with Cream

4 suprêmes of chicken or
  boned chicken breasts
6 tablespoons unsalted butter
2 very thick slices of white
  bread, cut into cubes
  (for croûtons) or 2 regular
  slices of white bread, crusts
  removed and cut into
  triangles (for croûtes)
salt and pepper
pinch of ground mace or
  nutmeg
$\frac{1}{4}$ cup sherry
1 cup heavy cream

This chicken can be cooked in
a skillet and served on a
platter, or cooked and served
in a shallow flameproof casserole.

Method

Melt half the butter in a skillet
or flameproof casserole and
fry the croûtons or croûtes
until golden; drain them on
paper towels and keep warm.

Place suprêmes or breasts
between 2 pieces of wax
paper and pound to flatten
them slightly.

Melt remaining butter, then
fry chicken gently for 10—15
minutes or until lightly brown
on both sides and very tender.
Season, add mace or nutmeg
and flame with the sherry.
Continue to cook, uncovered,
until the sherry has evaporated to a sticky glaze.

Add the cream, lower the
heat, cover and bring just to a
boil, shaking the pan so the
glaze dissolves. Arrange on a
platter or leave in the casserole and serve with croûtons
or croûtes.

Kidneys Chasseur

4 veal kidneys
$\frac{1}{4}$ lb piece of bacon, cut in cubes,
  blanched and drained
3 tablespoons butter
2 shallots, finely chopped
1 cup ($\frac{1}{4}$ lb) mushrooms, sliced
1 tablespoon flour
$\frac{1}{2}$ cup white wine
$\frac{1}{2}$ cup veal or chicken stock
1 teaspoon Dijon-style mustard
2 teaspoons tomato paste
salt and pepper

If kidneys are not available,
use veal escalopes for this
dish.

Method

Peel skin from the kidneys and
cut away as much of the core
as possible. In a skillet melt
half the butter and brown the
kidneys lightly on both sides —
do not use too high a heat;
remove them.
Watchpoint: kidneys must
always be cooked gently or
they will become hard; when
sliced they should be pink
inside.

Add remaining butter and
bacon to the pan with the
shallot and sauté gently for
1—2 minutes until the shallot
is soft. Add the mushrooms
and cook 2—3 minutes more
until all the moisture has
evaporated.

Stir in flour, pour in wine
and stock and bring to a boil,
stirring. Add mustard and
tomato paste with seasoning
and replace the kidneys.
Cover and cook just at simmering point for 10—15 minutes. Take out kidneys and cut
in $\frac{1}{4}$ inch slices.

Boil the sauce to reduce it
and taste for seasoning.
Arrange kidneys in a serving
dish, spoon over the sauce
and serve.

Pancakes à la Crème

8 pancakes (4—5 inches each) —
  see Volume 9
2 packages (6 oz) cream cheese
1 tablespoon sugar
$\frac{1}{2}$ teaspoon vanilla
$\frac{3}{4}$ cup heavy cream
$\frac{1}{2}$ cup dark cherry or blueberry
  jam, warmed

Method

Beat the cream cheese with
the sugar, vanilla and half the
cream. Spread this on 4 pancakes, and place the remaining pancakes on top. Stiffly
whip the remaining cream,
spoon over the pancakes and
broil them until they are
browned.

Top each pancake with a
spoonful of warmed jam and
serve immediately.

Macaroons with Orange

8 large macaroons
$\frac{1}{4}$ cup Curaçao, Grand Marnier,
  Triple Sec or other orange
  liqueur
1 dessert pear or 1 ripe peach

For orange cream
1 orange
6—8 sugar cubes
1 cup heavy cream
little granulated sugar
  (optional)

Method

Spread the macaroons on a
dish and sprinkle them with
the liqueur; leave 5—10 minutes.

Rub sugar cubes over the
orange rind until they are
saturated with the zest (oil).
Crush them and dissolve in
1—2 tablespoons juice from
the orange. Whip the cream,
and when it starts to thicken,

gradually beat in the orange
syrup with more sugar to
taste, if you like. The cream
should be thick enough to coat
a spoon but do not overbeat it.

Pare the pear, core and cut
it into 8 slices or scald, peel
and cut the peach in 8 slices,
discarding the pit.

Arrange the macaroons on
4 dessert plates, top each
with 2 slices of pear or peach
and coat with the orange
cream.

Pêches Farcies (Stuffed Peaches)

4 large ripe peaches, scalded,
  peeled and halved or 1 can
  (16 oz) peach halves
$\frac{1}{2}$ cup crushed macaroons
1 tablespoon Curaçao, Grand
  Marnier, Triple Sec or other
  orange liqueur
grated rind and juice of $\frac{1}{2}$ orange
1 tablespoon sugar
1 cup heavy cream

An alternative way of making
this dish is to soak the macaroons in kirsch and coat the
peaches with Melba sauce
instead of cream.

Method

Take the pits out of the
peaches. Soak the crushed
macaroons with the liqueur,
spoon into each peach cavity
and reshape by putting the
2 halves together.

Mix the orange rind and
juice with the sugar and stir
until the sugar dissolves.

Whip the cream and, when
it starts to thicken, gradually
beat in the orange syrup.
When the cream is of coating
consistency, spoon it over the
peaches and serve as soon as
possible.

Gazpacho, a piquant Spanish soup served cold, is a refreshing appetizer (recipe is on page 110)

MENU WITH A EUROPEAN FLAVOR

Gazpacho
or
Eggs Basquaise

Roast Pork Dijonnaise
Casserole of Onions & Potatoes

Apricot & Almond Strudel

Red wine – Rioja (Spain)
or Charbono (California)

This international menu begins with the hot-weather favorite, Spanish gazpacho – a piquant cold soup – followed by pork roast with a mustard topping in the French style, and a traditional strudel from Austria.

The gazpacho soup, flavored with tomato, suggests a Spanish wine and there is no reason why it should not suit the entrée. Distinguished red wines are now coming here from the Rioja district in north Spain. The best of these combine the elegance and authority of a good Bordeaux and, as they are still quite inexpensive, you can seek out the oldest vintages from the best producers. Charbono is a California wine of Italian heritage but, like the Rioja, it should have the full flavor required by the mustard-flavored pork roast.

TIMETABLE

Day before
Make and bake strudel and keep in an airtight container.
Hardcook eggs but do not peel; make dressing for eggs Basquaise but do not assemble.

Morning
Make gazpacho but do not add ice water; cover and refrigerate. Put remaining diced cucumber and green pepper in plastic wrap and seal tightly.
Prepare and cook onions and potatoes for casserole. Make sauce for pork and strain. Cook and add mushrooms and keep in refrigerator.
Prepare pork for roasting.

Assemble ingredients for final cooking from 6:00 for dinner around 8 p.m.

You will find that **cooking times** given in the individual recipes for these dishes have sometimes been adapted in the timetable to help you when cooking and serving this menu as a party meal.

Order of Work

6:00
Set oven at moderately hot (375°F) for pork.
Whip cream to serve with strudel.

6:15
Put pork in oven.
Assemble eggs Basquaise and garnish.

6:45
Baste pork.

7:15
Baste pork again.

7:35
Make croûtons for gazpacho.

7:45
Reheat onion and potato casserole on top of stove. Reheat sauce for pork. Add ice water to gazpacho, taste for seasoning and spoon into bowls. Arrange diced cucumber, green pepper and croûtons in small bowls. Put ice cubes in a bowl.
Transfer pork to a serving dish and keep warm.

8:00
Serve appetizer.
After serving appetizer, put strudel in moderate oven (350°F) to reheat, if you like.

Gazpacho

1 cup fresh white breadcrumbs
2–3 tablespoons red wine vinegar (or to taste)
2 cucumbers, peeled, seeded and diced
1 onion, diced
2 cloves of garlic, crushed
1 green pepper, cored, seeded and diced
½ cup olive oil
5–6 ripe tomatoes, coarsely chopped and worked through a sieve
salt
black pepper, freshly ground
1–2 cups ice water

For serving
3 slices of toasted bread, crusts removed, diced (for croûtons)

In Spain, ice cubes are added to this traditional soup just before serving.

Method
Soak the crumbs in 2 tablespoons vinegar. Put 1 diced cucumber, the onion, garlic and half the diced green pepper with the crumbs in a blender and work until smooth. Alternatively, work the mixture into a paste in a mortar and pestle, then work the paste through a fine sieve. Beat in the oil a few drops at a time, as in making mayonnaise, stir in the puréed tomatoes and season to taste, adding a little more vinegar, if needed. Chill thoroughly.

Just before serving, stir in the ice water – the amount depends on the juiciness of the tomatoes, but the soup should have a fairly thin consistency. Season to taste and serve in bowls with remaining diced cucumber, green pepper, and croûtons in separate dishes as garnish. A bowl of ice cubes also should be served separately.

Eggs Basquaise

6–8 eggs, hard-cooked and sliced
4 tomatoes, peeled and sliced
3–4 slices of canned pimiento, drained and cut in strips

For dressing
1 teaspoon paprika
1 teaspoon tomato paste
½ clove of garlic, crushed
2 tablespoons red wine vinegar
5 tablespoons oil
salt
black pepper, freshly ground
little sugar (optional)
2 tablespoons heavy cream

Method
To make dressing: mix paprika and tomato paste, add crushed garlic and mix to a paste. Stir in vinegar, then whisk in oil and taste for seasoning. Add a little sugar if dressing is too sharp.

Arrange eggs, tomatoes and pimientos in layers in a serving dish, reserving several strips of pimiento for decoration; moisten the layers using about two-thirds of the dressing. Finish with a layer of egg slices. Stir cream into remaining dressing and spoon over the top of the dish.

Decorate top with a lattice of pimiento strips and serve with breadsticks or crackers.

Arrange sliced pimientos, tomatoes and hard-cooked eggs in layers for eggs Basquaise; moisten with dressing

Eggs Basquaise, in a cream dressing, are decorated with lattice of pimiento strips

Roast pork Dijonnaise, with a crusty topping, is delicious with a casserole of onions and potatoes

Entrée

Roast Pork Dijonnaise

3 lb pork loin
1 tablespoon Dijon-style
    mustard
1 teaspoon sugar
1–1½ tablespoons white wine
¼ cup dry white breadcrumbs
12–14 whole cloves

For sauce
1 small onion, finely chopped
2½ tablespoons butter
1 tablespoon flour
1½ cups well-flavored stock
½ cup white wine
2 teaspoons tomato paste
2 cups (½ lb) mushrooms, sliced
salt and pepper

Method
Set oven at moderately hot
(375°F).

Trim excess fat from the
meat, leaving about a ½ inch
layer. Mix mustard, sugar and
wine to a paste, spread over
the pork, press on the crumbs
and stud the meat with cloves.

Put meat on a rack in a
roasting pan and roast in
heated oven for 1¾ hours or
until a meat thermometer
inserted in the meat registers
185°F. Baste the meat about
every 20 minutes during
cooking.

To prepare the sauce: cook
the onion in 1½ tablespoons
butter until soft but not brown,
stir in the flour and cook until
the mixture is well browned.
Stir in the stock, wine and
tomato paste and bring to a
boil. Simmer the sauce for
12–15 minutes or until it is
the consistency of light cream,
strain and return to the pan.

Sauté mushrooms in
remaining butter for 1 minute
or until just tender, add them

to the sauce and taste for
seasoning.

Arrange meat on a platter
and serve the sauce separately. Serve with a casserole
of onions and small new
potatoes.

*Spread the pork loin with a
paste of mustard, sugar and
wine, then press on the crumbs*

*Baste the pork loin, studded
with whole cloves, about
every 20 minutes during
cooking*

Accompaniment to entrée

Casserole of Onions and Potatoes

18–24 very small onions,
    blanched and peeled
6–8 small new potatoes,
    scraped, or 3 medium
    potatoes, peeled, quartered
    and sharp edges trimmed
2 tablespoons butter
1 teaspoon sugar
1 cup stock
1 tablespoon chopped parsley

Method
Put the onions in a flameproof
casserole with butter, sugar
and stock. Bring to a boil and
simmer 15–20 minutes or
until onions are tender and the
stock is reduced to about 2
tablespoons.

Watchpoint: do not let the
onions brown because this
will spoil both the flavor and
appearance of the finished
dish.

Cook potatoes in boiling
salted water for 12–20 minutes or until tender. Drain
and add them to the onions
with the parsley; stir carefully
until mixed. Serve in the
casserole.

*Casserole of onions and potatoes is garnished with chopped
parsley*

Apricot and almond strudel is delicious served warm with lightly whipped cream

Dessert

Apricot and Almond Strudel

1 lb fresh ripe apricots or
   1 can (16 oz) apricot halves
6 tablespoons sugar (optional)
$\frac{1}{2}$ cup heavy cream, whipped
   until it holds a soft shape
   (for serving)

For almond filling
$\frac{1}{2}$ cup whole blanched almonds,
   ground
$\frac{1}{4}$ cup sugar
$\frac{1}{2}$ a lightly beaten egg
2 tablespoons heavy cream

For strudel dough
$1\frac{1}{2}$–2 cups flour
pinch of salt
1 small egg
2 teaspoons oil
$\frac{1}{2}$ cup warm water
4–6 tablespoons melted butter
   (for brushing)
confectioners' sugar (for
   sprinkling)

Method

To make strudel dough: sift $1\frac{1}{2}$ cups of the flour into a bowl with salt and make a well in the center. Beat the egg, add oil and warm water and pour into the well. Work together to make a smooth elastic dough, adding more flour, if necessary, so the dough is soft but not sticky.

Knead dough 5 minutes, cover with an inverted bowl and leave in a warm place for 10–15 minutes. Set oven at hot (400°F).

To make the filling: cut fresh apricots in half, remove the pits and mix the halves with 6 tablespoons sugar; or drain canned apricots thoroughly. Mix ground almonds, sugar, egg and cream together to make a

smooth paste.

Roll dough out to $\frac{1}{4}$ inch thickness and lift onto a large floured cloth spread out on a table. (Cloth and table should be at least 3 feet square.) Leave 7–10 minutes for the dough to lose its elasticity.

Stretch the dough very gently, pulling the edges with both hands until it is paper-thin — it is easier for 2 people to do this. If you are alone, hold down 1 side with the rolling pin while pulling the other; the dough should be almost transparent.

Brush dough carefully with melted butter and spread with the almond mixture. Scatter the fresh sugared apricots or drained canned apricots over the top. Roll up the strudel by tilting the cloth so the dough turns upon itself.

Tip the dough onto a greased baking sheet, form into a horseshoe shape, brush with melted butter and bake in heated oven for 30–40 minutes or until crisp and browned.

Take from oven and cool slightly. Sprinkle with confectioners' sugar and serve strudel warm with a bowl of lightly whipped cream.

For strudel dough, work the egg and oil mixture with the flour to make a smooth elastic dough

After rolling out, place the strudel dough on a floured cloth and stretch it gently by pulling the edges; it should be almost transparent

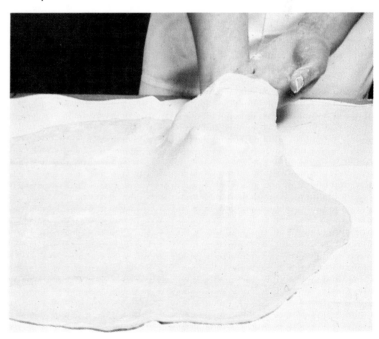

Serve ham and cream cheese rolls around a mound of celery curls, and garnish the cheese loaf with radish roses (see page 118)

COLD HORS D'OEUVRE AND APPETIZERS

Any party is half the work and twice the pleasure if you can prepare for it ahead of time.

Here are some tempting recipes to help you plan your next party — many will double as hors d'œuvre for cocktails or as appetizers for dinner according to your need. The scallop salad is substantial enough to serve as the entrée for a light lunch.

Cheese Loaf

1 lb loaf unsliced white bread
1 lb loaf unsliced wholewheat bread
5 cups (1¼ lb) finely grated mild Cheddar cheese
¼–½ cup scalded milk
⅓ cup unsalted butter, softened
salt and pepper
bunch of watercress, finely chopped
5–6 hard-cooked eggs, chopped
2 cups (½ lb) finely chopped or ground cooked ham
2–3 tablespoons chili sauce

For garnish
radish roses
small cress or watercress

Pastry bag and medium star tube

If possible use bread that is 1–2 days old – this makes the loaf easier to cut and spread. This recipe makes 2 cheese loaves; they freeze well so they can be stored for future occasions. Serve as an hors d'œuvre or appetizer.

Method

Remove crusts from both loaves and cut each loaf lengthwise – make 4 wholewheat and 6 white slices. Add enough scalded milk to the grated cheese to make a smooth mixture, beating it well. Beat in ¼ cup of the softened butter, season well and reserve two-thirds of the mixture. Divide remaining third in half, add finely chopped watercress to 1 portion and chopped hard-cooked eggs to the other; reserve them.

Work ham to a paste with chili sauce and beat in remaining softened butter.

To make 2 cheese loaves: cover 2 slices of white bread with half the watercress mixture; top each with a layer of wholewheat bread and spread with the ham filling. Add another layer each of white bread, spread with the egg mixture and top with a layer of wholewheat bread. Spread this with remaining watercress mixture and add the last slices of white bread. Press each loaf well, place a board and a weight on top and chill until firm.

Spread the top and sides of the loaves with some of the reserved cheese mixture, smoothing it with a metal spatula. Fill remaining cheese

For cheese loaf spread the watercress mixture on white bread, add a layer of wholewheat bread; then spread with ham and chili sauce mixture

Pipe the reserved cheese mixture to decorate the top edges of finished cheese loaf

mixture into the pastry bag fitted with the star tube and decorate the top of the loaves. Set them on a platter and garnish with radish roses and small cress or watercress. Chill well.

To serve: cut in thin slices. This can be made the day before.

Ham and Cream Cheese Rolls

½ lb cooked ham, sliced
1 package (8 oz) cream cheese
3–4 tablespoons hot milk
1 medium dill pickle, chopped
1 slice of canned pimiento, drained and chopped
salt and pepper
bunch of celery (for garnish)

Toothpicks

Serve as an hors d'œuvre.

Method

Cut celery into 2 inch thin sticks and soak in ice water for 1 hour or until curled.

Cut each slice of ham in half. Beat cream cheese with the hot milk until soft, add dill pickle and pimiento and sea-

For ham and cheese rolls, fill the sliced ham with the cheese mixture and roll up

son to taste. Put a spoonful of this mixture on each piece of ham, roll up and fasten with a toothpick. Arrange the rolls around a platter, drain the celery and pile in the center.

These can be made the day before.

Liptauer Cheese

1 cup cottage cheese
1 cup butter, softened
4 anchovy fillets, chopped
2 teaspoons caraway seeds
1 tablespoon chopped capers
1 tablespoon chopped chives
1 tablespoon paprika
2 teaspoons prepared mustard
1 teaspoon salt
½ teaspoon celery salt

Serve as an hors d'œuvre.

Method

Sieve the cottage cheese and beat in the softened butter. Mix in remaining ingredients, adding more of any seasonings as you like. Refrigerate for at least 24 hours.

Serve in a dish with savory Danish bread (see page 125), kartoffelstangen (see page 121), cheese straws or crackers.

Cheese Palmiers

1½ cup quantity of puff pastry,
or trimmings (see page 19)
1 cup grated Parmesan cheese

Serve as an hors d'oeuvre or
appetizer.

Method

Roll out pastry dough to a
rectangle 3 times as long as it
is wide, sprinkle with half the
cheese and fold in three. Roll
out again, sprinkle with remaining cheese, fold again
and chill for at least 30 minutes.

Set oven at hot (425°F).

Roll out dough to a 10 inch
square about ¼ inch thick.
Fold edge nearest to you
twice over to reach center of
dough. Repeat this from other
side, press lightly with a
rolling pin and fold one rolled
section of dough on top of the
other. Press again so dough
forms the shape of a heart
lying on its side, then with a
sharp knife cut across into
three-eighths to half inch
slices.

Place palmiers, flat sides
down, on a dampened baking
sheet leaving room for them
to spread. Open slices slightly
and flatten with the heel of
your hand to a palm leaf
shape. Bake in heated oven
for 10–12 minutes or until
brown on one side, then turn
and brown on other side for
about 7 minutes.

Serve hot or cold as an
appetizer with tomato salad or
a hot cream soup.

To serve as an hors d'oeuvre:
roll dough into a rectangle, cut
rectangle in half lengthwise
and fold as before so the
finished palmiers are much
smaller. These can be made
the day before.

Note: sweet palmiers recipe
was given in Volume 8.

*Pastry for palmiers is folded
over towards center and
flattened to the characteristic
palm leaf shape before baking*

Feuilletées

2 cup quantity of puff pastry
(see page 19)
1¼–1½ cups (10–12 oz)
Roquefort cheese
1 egg, beaten with ½ teaspoon
salt (for glaze)

Serve as an hors d'œuvre or
appetizer.

Method

Set oven at hot (425°F).

Roll out pastry dough to a
16 X 8 inch rectangle and cut
it in half lengthwise. Cut the
Roquefort into 8 rectangles
about 3 X 1 inch. Brush one
piece of dough with egg glaze
and lay the pieces of cheese
on top, about 1 inch apart,
leaving a ½ inch border.

Set the remaining piece of
dough on top and press it well
down between each piece of
cheese. Brush the top with
egg glaze and cut between
each piece of cheese to form
sticks. Set on a dampened
baking sheet and chill 15
minutes. Bake in heated oven
for 15–20 minutes until
puffed and brown. Serve hot

or cold as an appetizer.

To serve as an hors d'œuvre:
cut cheese into 1 inch squares
before placing on dough to
make small, square feuilletées.

These can be made the day
before and reheated on a
baking sheet in a moderately
hot oven (375°F) for 5–8
minutes.

Crab Ramekins

¾ lb backfin crab meat
½ envelope gelatin
¼ cup sherry
1 can consommé
2 teaspoons tomato paste

4 ramekins or individual dishes

Serve as an appetizer.

Method

Sprinkle gelatin over sherry
in a small pan and let stand
5 minutes or until spongy.
Melt over a pan of hot water
and stir into the consommé
with tomato paste.

Pile crab meat into dishes
with a fork so it does not
become tightly packed; spoon
over consommé. Cover and
chill at least 1 hour until set.

Serve with hot toast or
savory Danish bread (recipe
on page 125), if you like.
Make and serve the same day.

Crab Meat Dip

2 cups (1 lb) crab meat
1 can (8 oz) water chestnuts,
drained and chopped
2 tablespoons soy sauce
½ cup mayonnaise
1 tablespoon chopped fresh
ginger root
6–8 crab claws (for garnish) –
optional (for dipping)
bread sticks (for serving)
celery sticks (for serving)

Method

Combine all the ingredients,
pile in a bowl and chill.
Garnish with crab claws, if
you like, and serve bread
sticks and celery sticks for
dipping.

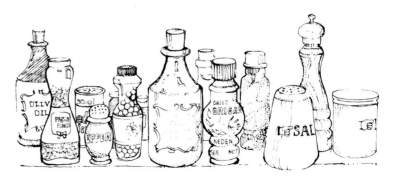

Stuffed clams, served in the half shell, make a very decorative centerpiece

Stuffed Clams with Parmesan

2 quarts clams, any kind
2 tablespoons butter
2 shallots or scallions, finely chopped
2 cloves of garlic, crushed
1 tablespoon chopped parsley
thick mornay sauce made with
    2 tablespoons butter,
    2 tablespoons flour, $\frac{3}{4}$ cup milk, $\frac{1}{4}$ cup grated Parmesan cheese, $\frac{1}{2}$ teaspoon prepared mustard, salt and pepper
2 tablespoons browned breadcrumbs
$\frac{1}{4}$ cup grated Parmesan cheese
2 tablespoons melted butter

This recipe can also be made with $1\frac{1}{2}$ cups canned chopped clams, instead of fresh clams. Prepare the clam mixture in the same way, fill it into 4 scallop shells or a baking dish and bake in a moderate oven (350°F) for 15–20 minutes or until browned. Serve as an appetizer.

Method
Scrub the clams thoroughly and discard any that do not close when tapped. Put them in a kettle, with a little salt and $\frac{1}{2}$ inch of water, cover and cook over high heat for 6–8 minutes or until clams open, stirring once. Remove the meat, reserving the shells, discard the black outer webbing on the necks, if using soft-shell clams, and chop meat finely. Discard any clams that do not open.

In a small pan melt the butter and sauté the shallots or scallions until soft. Take from the heat and stir in the garlic, clams, and parsley. Make the mornay sauce, stir into the clam mixture and taste for seasoning.

Fill the cheese mixture into the clam shells and sprinkle with browned breadcrumbs and Parmesan cheese, combined with melted butter. Bake clams in a moderate oven (350°F) for 12–15 minutes or until golden brown. Let cool before serving.

Kartoffelstangen

2 medium potatoes, peeled
1 cup butter
2 cups flour
salt and pepper
1 egg yolk, beaten with
    1 tablespoon milk (for glaze)
dill or caraway seeds

Serve as an hors d'oeuvre. Makes about 40 potato sticks.

Method
Leave butter at room temperature in a warm bowl.

Boil potatoes until tender, drain and dry them thoroughly. Mash with a potato masher or fork until smooth, and then add to the butter. Sift in flour with plenty of salt and pepper and work mixture together, first with a small spatula and then with the hand until it forms a soft dough. Chill for at least 1 hour. Set oven at hot (400°F).

Roll out the chilled dough into a rectangle about $\frac{1}{2}$ inch thick on a lightly floured board and trim the edges.

Brush the dough with egg and milk glaze and sprinkle the top with dill or caraway seeds. Cut the dough into sticks $\frac{1}{2}$ inch wide and 3–4 inches long, and place on a baking sheet. Bake in heated oven for about 15–18 minutes or until golden brown and crisp. Cool on a wire rack.

Arrange on a platter to serve with savory dips, Liptauer cheese (see page 118) or taramasalata (see Volume 12).

Danish Tartlets

pie pastry (made with 1 cup flour, pinch of salt, $\frac{1}{3}$ cup butter, 2–3 tablespoons cold water)

For filling
1 jar ($7\frac{1}{2}$ oz) smoked cod's roe, or 1 jar (8 oz) tarama
$\frac{1}{4}$ cup unsalted butter, softened
juice of $\frac{1}{2}$ lemon
pepper, freshly ground
4–5 cherry tomatoes
2 tablespoons finely chopped browned almonds
4–5 ripe olives, cut in wedges (optional)

8–9 tartlet pans ($2\frac{1}{2}$–3 inches); 3–3$\frac{1}{2}$ inch cookie cutter

Serve as an hors d'œuvre or appetizer.

Method
Make pastry dough and chill 30 minutes. Roll out dough thinly and, using a cookie cutter that is $\frac{1}{2}$ inch larger than the tartlet pans, cut out circles.

Line pans and bake blind in a moderately hot oven (375°F) for 12–15 minutes or until golden brown. Cool tartlets, but leave in pans.

To prepare filling: beat cod's roe or tarama with the butter and add lemon juice and pepper to taste.

Fill pastry cases with the filling, set half a cherry tomato on top of each and sprinkle a border of chopped almonds around the edges. Remove tartlets from pans and serve as an appetizer.

To serve as an hors d'œuvre: make pastry cases in $1\frac{1}{2}$ inch tartlet molds, fill the cases with filling, sprinkle with almonds and top with a wedge of cherry tomato or ripe olive. Make and serve same day.

Deviled Croissants

$1\frac{1}{2}$ cup quantity of puff pastry, or trimmings (see page 19)

For filling
$\frac{1}{4}$ cup finely chopped ham
1 tablespoon finely chopped dill pickle
2 teaspoons mayonnaise
few drops of Tabasco
1 egg, beaten with $\frac{1}{2}$ teaspoon salt (for glaze)

Serve hot or cold as an hors d'œuvre or as an accompaniment to soups and salads. Deviled croissants may be made the day before. Makes 12 croissants.

Method
Set oven at hot (425°F).

To prepare filling: mix ham, dill pickle and mayonnaise together, season well with Tabasco and set aside.

Roll out pastry dough into a 6 X 9 inch rectangle, trim the edges and cut it into 3 inch squares.

Cut each square in half diagonally and put $\frac{1}{2}$ teaspoon of the filling on each triangle. Roll up, shape into a crescent, place on a dampened baking sheet and chill 15 minutes. Brush croissants with egg glaze and bake in heated oven for 12–15 minutes or until golden brown and crisp.

Tarama (salted fish roe in oil) is available in Middle Eastern and specialty food stores.

Camembert en surprise, garnished with radishes and pretzels, is an ideal accompaniment to cocktails

Camembert en Surprise

1 ripe Camembert cheese
$\frac{1}{3}$ cup unsalted butter
3 tablespoons white wine
$\frac{1}{4}$ cup dry white breadcrumbs
salt and pepper
8–12 radishes
$\frac{1}{3}$ cup whole blanched almonds,
   browned and ground
4 ripe olives, halved and
   pitted
6–8 pretzels
few sprigs of watercress
   (optional)

5–6 inch cake pan

Serve as an hors d'œuvre or appetizer.

Method
Line cake pan with a circle of wax paper.

Cut or scrape away the rind of the Camembert and work the cheese through a sieve.

Cream the butter, add cheese and work in the wine and breadcrumbs, a little at a time. Season to taste and spoon into the prepared pan. Cover with plastic wrap and chill 2–3 hours or until firm.

Cut the radishes into roses and leave them in ice water for 1–2 hours to open.

Loosen the edges of the cheese mold with a knife and turn it out into the browned ground almonds. Coat it all over with almonds, pressing them on with a knife and lift onto a platter. Mark the top into wedges with the back of a knife and decorate with olive halves. Press the pretzels around the cheese, drain radish roses and arrange around the platter with watercress to garnish.

Make the day before, chill and cut in wedges. Serve with unsalted crackers.

Roll Camembert mixture in the browned ground almonds

Press pretzels against the sides of almond-coated cheese

Tomatoes Bruxelloise

8 even-sized, medium
   tomatoes, peeled
salt and pepper
2 tablespoons heavy cream
$\frac{3}{4}$ cup mayonnaise
small clove of garlic, crushed
$\frac{1}{2}$ lb cooked, peeled shrimps,
   chopped
bunch of watercress (for
   garnish)

Serve as an appetizer.

Method
Cut off bottoms (not stem end) of tomatoes and reserve. Scoop out the seeds. Season the insides and reserve.

Stir cream into mayonnaise with garlic. Add shrimps, season to taste and spoon into the tomatoes, mounding well. Replace the lids.

Arrange on a platter or individual plates, and chill. Garnish with watercress. Make and serve the same day.

Shrimp Pâté

$\frac{1}{2}$ lb uncooked, peeled shrimps
$\frac{1}{2}$ cup butter
pinch of ground mace
dash of Tabasco
salt
black pepper, freshly ground
2 tablespoons sherry (optional)

*Soufflé dish or terrine (3 cup
   capacity), or 4 individual
   ramekins*

Serve as an appetizer.

Method
Melt half the butter in a skillet and sauté shrimps for 2–3 minutes, depending on size, until they are cooked and bright pink. Halfway through cooking, sprinkle the shrimps with mace, Tabasco, salt and plenty of pepper. When cooked, drain shrimps (reserve the butter), peel them and chop finely or work a few at a time in a blender. Mix with butter in which they were cooked and the sherry, if used, and taste for seasoning.

Pack into the dish, terrine or individual ramekins. Melt the remaining $\frac{1}{4}$ cup butter, pour it over the pâté to seal and chill. The pâté will keep, covered, in the refrigerator for 1–2 days.

Spoon portions onto individual plates or leave in ramekins and serve with hot toast.

Scallop Salad

1 lb sea scallops, drained and
   cut in 2–3 even-sized pieces
juice of 3 lemons
2 tablespoons oil
1 cup plain yogurt
2 teaspoons tarragon
salt and pepper
$\frac{1}{2}$ cup finely chopped walnuts
1 cucumber, peeled, seeded
   and cut in julienne strips
lettuce leaves (for garnish)

Serve as an appetizer or light entrée.

Method
Put scallops in a china or glass dish, pour over two-thirds of the lemon juice, cover and refrigerate 8–12 hours, stirring occasionally. Drain scallops thoroughly on paper towels.

Beat oil into yogurt with remaining lemon juice, tarragon and seasoning to taste. Add scallops to walnuts and cucumber and mix with yogurt dressing.

Pile salad on lettuce leaves, set on individual plates and serve chilled with savory Danish bread, if you like (see page 125).

Start preparing the salad the day before; make dressing and finish it the morning before.

Savory Danish bread is sprinkled with poppy seeds and Parmesan cheese

Savory Danish Bread

3 cups flour
1 cup butter
1 cup lukewarm milk
$\frac{1}{2}$ teaspoon salt
2 tablespoons sugar
1 cake compressed or
 1 package dry yeast
1 egg, beaten to mix

For filling
1 large onion, finely chopped
$\frac{1}{4}$ cup butter
3 tablespoons fresh white
 breadcrumbs
2 tablespoons whole blanched
 almonds, ground
2 tablespoons grated Parmesan
 cheese
1 egg, beaten to mix
salt and pepper

To finish
1 tablespoon grated Parmesan
 cheese
1 tablespoon poppy or sesame
 seeds

10 inch tube pan

Serve as an hors d'oeuvre, cut in slices and with a dip. Or serve as an appetizer with soups and salads. The bread may be make 1–2 days ahead.

Method
To prepare dough: melt $\frac{1}{4}$ cup butter in the milk. Cool to lukewarm. Sift flour with salt into a bowl and make a well in the center. Pour in the warm milk, add sugar and sprinkle over yeast. Let stand 5 minutes or until yeast is dissolved. Stir in beaten egg and mix to a smooth dough with the hand.

Knead in bowl for 5 minutes or until dough is smooth and elastic. Cover and let rise in a warm place for 1 hour or until almost doubled in bulk.

Work dough to knock out air, turn it out on a floured board and knead lightly until smooth. Roll out to an 18 X 6 inch rectangle and cover two-thirds of the dough with half the remaining butter, divided into small pieces. Fold in three and roll as for flaky or puff pastry. Fold in three and roll again. Put on remaining butter, fold and chill 15 minutes. Roll and fold twice more, cover with plastic wrap and chill 30 minutes or until firm. **Watchpoint**: if dough starts to stick at any stage during rolling, fold it and chill until firm before rolling again.

To make filling: cook onion in butter until golden and take from heat. Add breadcrumbs, ground almonds and cheese and bind with a little beaten egg, reserving the rest. Season well and let cool.

Lightly butter the tube pan and set oven at hot (400°F).

Roll out chilled dough to an 18 X 12 inch oblong, spread filling on top, roll up dough and join the ends to make a circle. Place in prepared tube pan and leave to rise in a warm place for 20–30 minutes or until almost doubled in bulk.

Brush with the reserved beaten egg, sprinkle with grated Parmesan cheese and poppy or sesame seeds and bake in heated oven for 45–50 minutes or until the bread sounds hollow when tapped. Cool on a wire rack.

Roll out the bread dough to an oblong, then spread with cheese filling and roll up

Cassolettes of Cucumber

6–7 cucumbers
9–10 slices of bread (for croûtes)
$\frac{1}{2}$ cup butter (for frying) – optional
3 different fillings (see right)
2–3 slices of canned pimiento, cut in strips or rounds
2 cups aspic (see Volume 8)
watercress (for garnish)

2 inch plain cookie cutter; 1–1$\frac{1}{4}$ inch plain cookie cutter (optional)

Cassolettes are individual containers (little casseroles). In this recipe the cucumber cases take the place of true cassolettes. Serve as an hors d'oeuvre or appetizer.

Method
Score the cucumber peel lengthwise with a fork to make a ridged pattern. Cut cucumbers in 1 inch slices and cut out each center about halfway through with the smaller cookie cutter or small sharp knife. Scoop out some of the seeds to leave each cucumber case with a base. Blanch the cases in boiling salted water for 5 minutes, then drain, refresh and drain again. Prepare the fillings (see right).

To make croûtes: toast bread and cut 4 circles from each slice with larger cookie cutter, or cut out circles and fry them in butter.

Place cucumber cases on croûtes and fill with different fillings, mounding them on top. Decorate with strips or rounds of pimiento and chill thoroughly. Brush with cool but still liquid aspic so the cases are glazed and top each with a sprig of watercress.

Make and serve chilled the same day.

Cassolette Fillings

Mushroom

1 cup ($\frac{1}{4}$ lb) finely chopped mushrooms
2 tablespoons butter
1 teaspoon flour
3–4 tablespoons milk or stock
salt and pepper
1 teaspoon chopped fresh mint

Method
Melt butter, add mushrooms and cook over medium heat for 3 minutes or until all the moisture has evaporated. Take from heat, stir in flour and pour in milk or stock. Season and cook mixture until it thickens. Add chopped mint and cool thoroughly before using.

Cheese and Shrimp

1 small package (3 oz) cream cheese
$\frac{1}{2}$ cup ($\frac{1}{4}$ lb) chopped, cooked and peeled shrimps
salt and pepper

Method
Work cream cheese until soft, add the shrimps and season to taste.

Chicken and Ham or Tongue

$\frac{1}{4}$ cup finely chopped cooked chicken
$\frac{1}{4}$ cup finely chopped cooked ham or tongue
1 anchovy fillet, finely chopped
1 tablespoon mayonnaise
salt and pepper

Method
Mix chicken, ham or tongue and anchovy and bind with the mayonnaise. Season well.

GARNISHES

Simple garnishes are often the most effective — a crisp bunch of watercress, a slice of lemon or a sprinkling of parsley can do as much for a dish as the most elaborate geometric arrangement of sliced truffles.

Garnishes should stimulate the appetite as well as the eye; they should complement the flavor of the dish they adorn as well as highlighting its color. And most important of all — a garnish must always be edible.

Below, we give some easy-to-prepare garnishes that will enhance your finished dishes.

  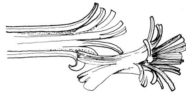

Artichoke Bottoms
If using large artichokes, cut off the stalks and pull away the lower leaves. Cut the tops off remaining leaves, leaving about 1 inch at the base. Cook artichokes in boiling salted water for 20–25 minutes or until tender, drain and cool slightly.

Pull away the leaves and scoop out the hairy chokes with a teaspoon. Trim the bottom neatly and, if the cavity in the center is not deep enough, scoop out a little of the heart.

Fill with sauce, fresh tomato purée, cooked small vegetables such as peas (see recipe for tournedos Parisienne on page 54), or salad.

Carrot Curls
Peel a long carrot with a vegetable peeler. Cut the carrot in half lengthwise, then with the peeler cut thin broad strips down cut length of carrot. Wrap these pliable strips loosely around your index finger, slip off, secure with a toothpick. Keep curls in a bowl of ice water until needed. Remove toothpicks before using.

Celery or Scallion Brushes
Cut stalks of celery into sections about 2 inches long. With a sharp knife cut very thin slices about one-third of the way down both ends of the celery. Place in ice water for the celery to curl — the thinner the slices, the curlier the 'brush'.

For scallions, cut off the root and trim the stalk to make about 2 inch lengths. With a sharp knife cut thin slivers through both stalk and root end so the slivers are held together in the middle. Toss in ice water for curly brush or fringe effect.

Cucumber Turns
Score a firm cucumber with the prongs of a fork to make striped pattern, then cut in thin, uniform slices. Make a cut in each slice from center to edge. Twist one cut edge away from center to make slices stand up.

Thin slices of **lemons**, **limes** and **oranges** can also be 'turned' in this way.

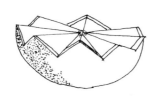

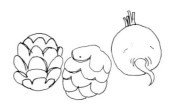

Lemon Butterflies
Cut a lemon in medium slices and cut each slice in half. Starting at the rind side, cut each slice almost to the center and force these cuts apart so the half slice forms 'wings'. A piece of parsley placed in the center of the 'wings' makes the butterfly's body.

Notched Lemons
Stand the lemon on its broad base. With a small sharp knife cut a band of deep inverted 'V's around the middle, slicing through to center of fruit. Pull halves apart and sprinkle the surface with finely chopped parsley, paprika or whatever makes a good color contrast.

Limes, oranges, grapefruit, tomatoes and **hard-cooked eggs** can be 'notched'.

Radish Roses
Trim tails and all but smallest green leaves from red radishes. With a sharp knife, make several angled cuts like tiny petals down the radish, starting at root end and working down to stem end; do not slice completely through. Or, make several vertical cuts from root to stem end, again not slicing completely through. Keep radishes in a bowl of ice water to open out petals before using.

Tomato, Lemon, Lime or Orange Baskets
Choose the most attractive fruit you can find and cut a thin slice from the bottom so that it will stand upright. With a small sharp knife, remove nearly a whole quarter-section from each fruit, leaving a strip wide enough for handle of basket. Remove the other quarter-section from opposite half of fruit. Cut away flesh underneath handle to hollow out fruit. Basket edges can be left plain or notched; they may also be sprinkled with finely chopped parsley or paprika. The basket will hold a sauce, small cooked vegetables or cut-up fruits.

Lemon Knots
Cut the lemon in half crosswise and cut a thin slice from each end so the halves will stand upright. Pare a thin strip of rind from the cut edge of each half, but do not detach. Make a knot in each strip of rind so it stands out.

Pickle Fans
With a sharp knife cut thin slices down the length of small sweet or gherkin pickles, leaving them joined at one end. Spread slices apart into a fan.

Tomato Roses
With a sharp knife, start at the stem end of a small firm tomato; cut a strip of peel about 1 inch wide into a long spiral, including a little flesh. Use a sawing motion while cutting to make strip wavy. Then gently wind strip around and around, holding bottom part of rose a little tighter than the top; this way the top will blossom like the real flower.

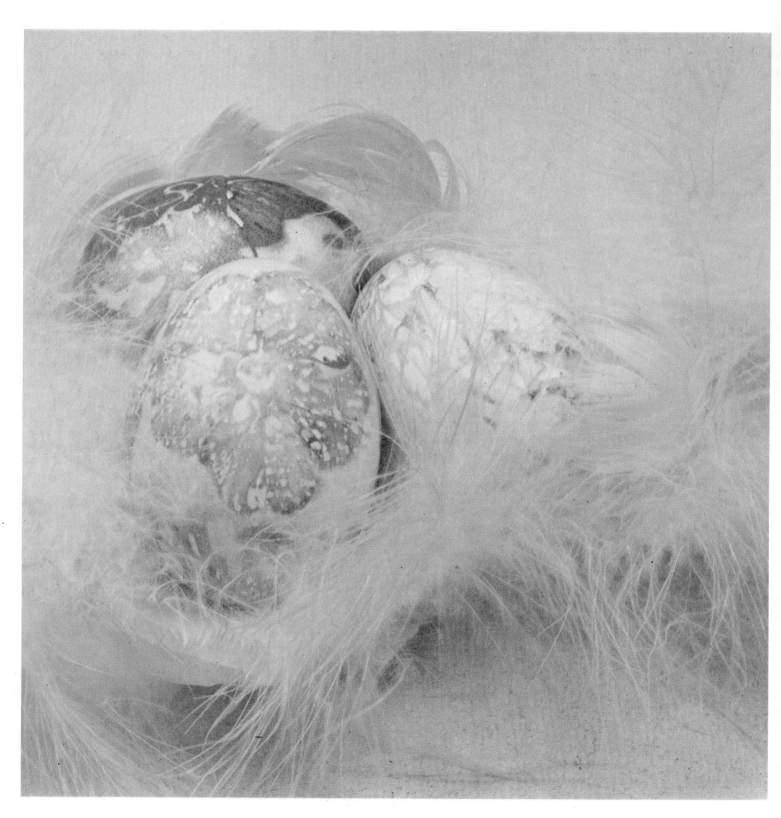

EASTER EGGS

Fancifully decorated and colorful Easter eggs are the traditional symbols of new life, linked to the arrival of spring.

The use of the egg in seasonal celebrations dates back to pagan spring festivals. In ancient Egypt, eggs were considered to come from the hare (a symbol of fertility), whose North American counterpart is the Easter rabbit.

Adopted by Christianity, the egg came to represent resurrection and was often consecrated for ceremonial use in churches. For hundreds of years, eggs were banned as a food during Lent by church law, then welcomed back on Easter Sunday, surrounded with local rituals that still survive.

In Greece for instance each person in a group bangs his red Easter egg against those of the others and proclaims the resurrection of Christ. Legend says that the red color recalls a miracle that occurred when a disbeliever saw white eggs change color before his eyes.

In Mexico eggs are blown through a pinhole at each end until empty, then filled with chocolate or perfume.

In some parts of northern England, colored eggs are rolled down slopes on Easter Monday. President Hayes revived the custom here when he invited a group of noisy children who had been chased from the Capitol Hill grounds to take their games to the White House lawn. Today children still carry their colored eggs in baskets to a party on Easter Monday on the same green acreage.

Since the pre-Christian days when eggs were first colored with simple dyes. Easter egg decoration has developed into an art. The ornate wax designs of Poland and the Ukraine are collectors' items. Engraving eggs of precious metals or glass with a steel point or diamond is reserved for skilled craftsmen. Examples of the renowned enamel and gold Easter eggs made by the 19th century jeweler, Fabergé, for the Russian court of St. Petersburg, recently sold at auction for several thousand dollars

DECORATING EASTER EGGS

Designing Easter eggs at home has become a tradition because it is one of the few remaining crafts that has not been taken over by machines. Even though machine-made chocolate Easter eggs have filled candy stores since Victorian times, the fragile natural shell must still be decorated by hand.

Preparation for Decoration

The basic procedures are simple. First the eggs are either hard-cooked or blown empty. Puncture a small hole in each end of an egg with a needle or sharp-pointed instrument, then slowly blow the contents through one end of the egg into a bowl. Rinse and dry the empty shell thoroughly. If you like, to make the egg less fragile, fill the empty shell with wax and reseal it with white wax. Although empty egg shells are more fragile, they do not have to be refrigerated like hard-cooked ones.

Hardcook eggs for 10–12 minutes, preferably in an enameled pan, with 1 teaspoon vinegar and $\frac{1}{4}$ teaspoon baking soda to clean the shell so the dye will coat evenly. Rinse in cool water, then place them, one at a time, in $\frac{1}{2}$ cup hot water combined with $\frac{1}{2}$–1 teaspoon food coloring for about 1 minute or until the desired color is obtained. Pick up the eggs with a large spoon and transfer them to a paper towel or

wire rack. Let them stand a few minutes until dry, then store them in the refrigerator if not to be used within a few hours.

Convenient and inexpensive dyeing kits are available in supermarkets and five and dime stores around Easter. These kits usually contain a selection of primary food color dyeing tablets, a wax marking pencil and a wire egg dipper. They often include transfer designs in Easter motifs, flowers, cartoons or border patterns. Tablets, like food coloring, can be mixed to obtain different shades, or one color can be dyed over another.

Kinds of Decoration

The wax writer serves the same purpose as a wax crayon or melted candle wax applied with a brush. When egg is dipped in slightly cooled dye, waxed portions do not color. In addition to simple patterns and drawings or names written in wax, you can create interesting effects by alternately drawing on the egg and dipping it into different colors. Wax-covered areas will retain the color of the dye process immediately preceding. And colors look cleaner if you work from light to dark shades, and vivid colors can be outlined in white.

Traditional Ukrainian Easter eggs are decorated in elaborate, bold, geometric designs. First mark the egg in half, lengthwise, and across the center with a pencil. Divide sections into triangles with wax and alternately dip egg into dye and mark new portions off with wax. Within the sections you can create different geometric patterns or perfectly symmetrical ones.

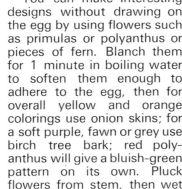

The traditional colors are yellow, orange, red, green, brown and black. Melt off protective coats of wax by holding egg beside a flame, rotating and wiping gently as the wax melts.

The Ukrainians save eggs decorated in this way for years. If kept out of direct sunlight, the colors will not fade.

A thin coating of colored wax creates a glowing opalescent veneer. Melt either one bright, or a mixture of colored, candle stubs in a pan of hot water. The wax will rise to the top of the water and a gentle swirling motion will create a rainbow-like layer. Dip egg through wax film, twirling as you dip. One word of caution: avoid mixing colors that combine to make a dreary grey. You can also make a dual-colored egg by using separate colors on each half.

Painting directly on the egg is one of the simplest and most effective decorating techniques. The flexibility in creating your own geometric or free-form designs is limitless. Painting is a quicker way to make Ukrainian-style patterns, using either food dyes or, for more intricate designs on blown eggs, oil paints and water colors. Dyed or painted eggs can be glazed by rubbing them with a little salad oil.

You can make interesting designs without drawing on the egg by using flowers such as primulas or polyanthus or pieces of fern. Blanch them for 1 minute in boiling water to soften them enough to adhere to the egg, then for overall yellow and orange colorings use onion skins; for a soft purple, fawn or grey use birch tree bark; red polyanthus will give a bluish-green pattern on its own. Pluck flowers from stem, then wet egg and place flowers on it to form a pattern. Hold in position or cover with onion skins or birch bark and while holding firmly, bandage tightly with 1-inch strips cut from any suitable cloth or bandage. Keep all in place with two rubber bands. Put egg into pan of cold water and bring gently to a boil, then simmer about 15 minutes. Cool in cold water, peel off bandage strips and wash if necessary.

You can add a dimension to Easter egg decoration by using a collage or appliqué. Attach fabrics like gingham or velvet (with or without ribbons, rickrack, buttons, beads, or sequins) with clear silicone glue available in hardware stores. Create patterns with pregummed stars or labels cut into shapes, brush eggs with dye, then remove shapes. Hold designs snipped from paper doilies against eggshell with pieces of masking tape and spray non-toxic paint from an Aerosol can for a silhouette effect. The eggs can be dyed first for added color.

If you plan to cover the entire surface of an egg, work on one half at a time. For example, if using cake-decorating silver sprinkles, first squeeze glue onto a small section of prepared shell and smooth over with a toothpick. Use tweezers to place silver sprinkles close together on shell. Continue until half the egg is covered, then dry overnight before completing the remaining half.

Before covering an eggshell with fabric, try slicing off the upper quarter to form a small basket to fill with flowers or homemade candies. Hang it on the branches of an 'Easter tree' that has been sprayed with silver or colored paint. First tap the egg with a knife near the pointed end and lift off the top. Then empty the contents, immediately trim shell with scissors. Do not let eggshell dry out or it will become brittle. Rinse and drain until dry. Mark prepared shell into lengthwise quarters with a pencil. Make a shield-shaped pattern for each section and work with one section at a time. Place a fine line of white glue down center of one quarter, then place gingham, calico or other fabric in position; hold for one minute or until firmly set, trimming any excess fabric. Lift sides of fabric and coat shell with a little glue; smooth over and remove excess. Repeat on remaining 3 quarters, then cover seams with 2 strips of ribbon, glued from one cut edge around to the other. To make a handle: extend one ribbon strip beyond the cut edge and glue to the opposite side. Finish with a border of lace extending a little above cut edge.

Any one or a combination of techniques — applied with imagination and care can transform the humble egg into a delightful decoration for Easter and all year.

MEASURING & MEASUREMENTS

The recipe quantities in the Course are measured in standard level teaspoons, tablespoons and cups and their equivalents are shown below. Any liquid pints and quarts also refer to U.S. standard measures.

When measuring dry ingredients, fill the cup or spoon to overflowing without packing down and level the top with a knife. All the dry ingredients, including flour, should be measured before sifting, although sifting may be called for later in the instructions.

Butter and margarine usually come in measured sticks (1 stick equals $\frac{1}{2}$ cup) and other bulk fats can be measured by displacement. For $\frac{1}{3}$ cup fat, fill the measuring cup $\frac{2}{3}$ full of water. Add fat until the water reaches the 1 cup mark. Drain the cup of water and the fat remaining equals $\frac{1}{3}$ cup.

For liquids, fill the measure to the brim, or to the calibration line.

Often quantities of seasonings cannot be stated exactly, for ingredients vary in the amount they require. The instructions 'add to taste' are literal, for it is impossible to achieve just the right balance of flavors in many dishes without tasting them.

Liquid measure	Volume equivalent
3 teaspoons	1 tablespoon
2 tablespoons	1 fluid oz
4 tablespoons	$\frac{1}{4}$ cup
16 tablespoons	1 cup or 8 fluid oz
2 cups	1 pint
2 pints	1 quart
4 quarts	1 gallon

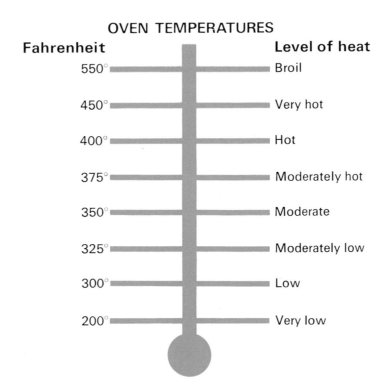

OVEN TEMPERATURES

Fahrenheit		Level of heat
550°		Broil
450°		Very hot
400°		Hot
375°		Moderately hot
350°		Moderate
325°		Moderately low
300°		Low
200°		Very low

OVEN TEMPERATURES AND SHELF POSITIONS

Throughout the Cooking Course, oven temperatures are stated in degrees Fahrenheit and in generally agreed levels of heat such as 'high' and 'moderate'. The equivalents are shown on the table above.

However, exact temperature varies in different parts of an oven and the thermostat reading refers to the heat in the middle. As the oven temperature at top and bottom can vary as much as 25°F from this setting, the positioning of shelves is very important. In general, heat rises, so the hottest part of the oven is at the top, but consult the manufacturer's handbook about your individual model.

Pans and dishes of food should be placed parallel with burners or elements to avoid scorched edges.

When baking cakes, there must be room for the heat to circulate in the oven around baking sheets and cake pans; otherwise the underside of the cakes will burn. If baking more than one cake in an oven that has back burners or elements, arrange the cakes side by side. If the oven has side burners, arrange cakes back and front.

Oven thermostats are often inaccurate and are unreliable at extremely high or low temperatures. If you do a great deal of baking or question the accuracy of your oven, use a separate oven thermometer as a check on the thermostat.

Cooking Curiosities

Although 'four and twenty blackbirds' baked in a pie would never be served to a king anymore, cakes and pastries that were made for special occasions and served to the English Tudors and Stuarts are still served today. Dating from the Elizabethan banquets that always ended with an elaborate confection in some suitable shape, festive cakes continue to play a major role in the celebration of any event.

Here, almost every traditional cake made for special occasions originated in England or Europe. The only real traditional American dessert is not even a cake but pumpkin pie, always served on Halloween and at Thanksgiving. Lady Baltimore cake also originated here and is usually served at large receptions with a glass of Champagne; it is a three-layered white cake sandwiched with white icing and figs, raisins and pecans. Election Day cake, a spicy coffeecake, comes from New England and was made for town meetings and elections in New England. Other American traditions — simnel cake for Mother's Day and Christmas cake for Christmas are carried on from England. There, such

occasions as the twelfth day of Christmas are marked by the baking of a special Twelfth Night cake, and the one illustrated here was made for Queen Victoria. The top is decorated with sixteen figures representing an 18th century picnic and a minstrel accompaniment.

The famous 18th century pastry chef, Carême, considered cake-making to be a branch of architecture, and he built pavilions, temples and rotundas from royal icing. He may well have been the chef who demanded that his master remove a portion of his ceiling to accommodate a particularly tall creation.

The French are also steeped in sweet traditions. They celebrate Christmas with an elaborately decorated Christmas log called a 'Buche de Noël', covered with vines and leaves formed from green-colored almond paste and mushrooms made from meringue. January 6, the Day of Epiphany, is marked by a 'Galette des Rois' (cake of Kings) made from puff pastry in which a bean is baked. The person in the family who finds the bean becomes a monarch and chooses his court for the day.

INDEX
(Volume 15)

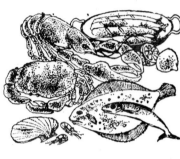

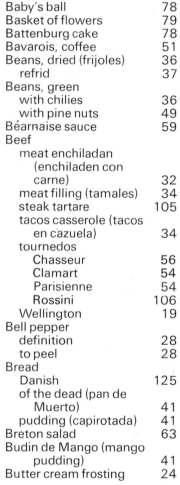

Acknowledgments
Photographs by Fred J. Maroon on pages 26, 29, 30, 33, 38, 42, 84 and 85. Photograph on page 108 by C. Délu/PAF. Other photographs by Michael Leale, John Ledger, Gina Harris and Roger Phillips.

NOTES